THE WAY OF THE HEART

TEACHINGS OF DHARMA
MASTER HSIN TAO

THE WAY OF THE HEART

TEACHINGS OF DHARMA

MASTER HSIN TAO

Published by:
CreateSpace Independent Publishing Platform
ISBN-13: 978-1530660131
Issue Date: 2016/09/05

From the reviews of the way of the heart

The Way of the Heart - This small four-chapter volume is a real treasure! Maria R. Habito, originally from Germany, made a pilgrimage to the East, and now shares with us in the West the treasures of meditation taught by the joyously radiant Buddhist Dharma Master Hsin Tao:

*how to sit contemplatively, body and mind
*how to stop our incessant flow of distracted thoughts
and emotions
*how to practice "deep listening to the silence"
which awakens the power of enlightenment within;
*how to see everything in the universe with new eyes,
releasing the flow of unconditional love and compassion.

Through Dharma Master Hsin Tao's book, the Marriage of East and West will continue to unfold until we truly awaken to our gifted Reality: we are One!

Sr. Pascaline Coff, osb
Benedictine Sisters of Perpetual Adoration
Clyde, Mo

Dharma Master Hsin-tao has given us a gem of a book. He explains the basic teachings of Buddhism and the Way of Chan (Zen) with a simplicity and depth that only a gifted teacher can offer. Best of all, the teachings are presented in light of this man's extraordinary story of being deprived of his parents, conscription as a child-soldier, life on the streets of Tai Pei and finally his quest for liberation by becoming a mountain ascetic. Highly recommended for undergraduates and graduate students.

Rev. James L. Fredericks, Ph.D
Theology Department, Loyola Marymount University, Los Angeles CA

Dharma Master Hsin Tao writes from the heart, and shares with us intimate moments and crucial turning-points in his journey from a war orphan to a global spiritual leader. Readers are led by the hand into the basic teachings of Buddhism addressing issues of human suffering, the causes of suffering, and the way to liberation from suffering. The author teaches by example, and shows us how to live the selfless life of a Bodhisattva in our twenty-first century global society.

Professor Ruben L.F. Habito
Guiding Teacher, Maria Kannon Zen Center, and author of Zen and the Spiritual Exercises: Paths of Awakening and Transformation (Orbis 2013) and Healing Breath: Zen for Christians and Buddhists in a Wounded World (Wisdom 2006)

Contents

INTRODUCTION

Ifirst met Dharma Master Hsin Tao in spring of 1980, when I was a student of Chinese language and religion at the Shifan University in Taipei. At that time, Shifu, as he is called by his disciples and friends, still lived at the hermitage on Dragon Lake near the town of Yilan on the East Coast of Taiwan. The hermitage consisted of a small building that contained a Buddhist shrine and Shifu's own room where he would spend most of the time in meditation, a simple kitchen just across the courtyard, and another small building towards the back where I was allowed to stay overnight, sharing the space with an elderly nun who prepared simple meals for us during my stays. The hermitage, called "Dreamlike Hut" was an oasis of tranquility, overlooking the lake that was deeply embedded in lush tropical vegetation.

At my first visit, I was struck by the clarity and inner peace that this young master radiated, and I wondered about its provenance. "Come back and visit as often as you would like to," Shifu told me as I was about to leave that evening. He then added that I was "a tree that can bring rich fruit if its roots are planted in the right soil," which only served to further confuse me and pique my interest. After some initial hesitation I did return to the hermitage often during weekends, where Shifu's questions about my self-understanding as a Christian proved to be very thought-provoking. A the same time, I always returned back to my studies in Taipei with a profound sense of peace and quiet joy, born from the simple fact of his presence. When I returned to Germany in the summer of 1981 to take up my studies of Chinese, Japanese, and Philosophy at the University of Munich, I seriously followed Shifu's advice to take up the practice of Zen meditation. "Otherwise," Shifu had told me, "you will write about Buddhism in an academic and intellectual way only, without any experiential understanding of the truth taught by the Buddha." When I returned to Taiwan in 1983 to attend a conference on Matteo Ricci, the Jesuit missionary who had entered China four hundred years earlier to bring the Christian teachings of the "Lord of Heaven" to the educated class of scholars and court officials under the Ming Dynasty, I had already started my own Zen practice at a Franciscan retreat house near Munich under the guidance of Father Enomiya Lassalle, the Jesuit missionary who had been introduced to Zen practice in Japan and brought it back as a great resource for Christians in Europe to deepen their spiritual path.

In the meanwhile, Shifu had moved from the hermitage to a cave on Ling Jiou Mountain where he was keeping a strict two-year ascetic regimen of meditating and fasting. Other than the cave, there was just a very small temple building, which is now called the "Founder's Hall" and a kitchen which is still in use today, albeit completely reconstructed and enlarged. In 1983, the road to the mountaintop did not yet exist, and I climbed up all the way on foot. Upon arrival, I was warmly greeting by the young nun Liaoyi shi, now the CEO of the Museum of World Religions, and brought to the cave to meet Shifu. At first glance I would not have recognized him—this emaciated figure with wild long hair reaching over his shoulders and a long, thin beard. This appearance, of course, was due to the fasting and fact that no bodily hair is trimmed during the period of the retreat. One look at his eyes however reassured me: they exuded the same depth and luminosity as before, perhaps even more so now.

Inviting me into the cave, Shifu told me in his quiet and familiar voice that in the future many, many people would be coming to Ling Jiou Mountain, and that he would be traveling all over the world to bring the teaching to those who have not yet heard of it and are longing for liberation from suffering. "I need your help in this," he added, to my surprise. "You have always understood me well and can translate what I say into many languages. You can help me reach so many people." Even while wondering how this could be, since nothing in Shifu's ascetic and eremitic lifestyle pointed towards world travel, I had the sense that he might be seeing into the future. And even though I hesitated at first to become his disciple and accept his invitation to undertake the Triple Refuge ceremony during my short visit, my hesitations were dispelled with Shifu's assurance that I could remain a Christian. "You do not take your refuge to a Buddha, dharma, and sangha outside, but to the enlightened nature of your own heart and mind," he said. To my own surprise I emerged from the Triple Refuge ceremony with a profound sense of joy and inner peace.

I returned to Germany to continue my studies at the University of Munich and later at Kyoto University, finishing with a Ph.D. in 1990. I moved to the US, got married, and bore two children. In the meantime, Shifu had come out of his retreat and established the Wu Sheng Monastery on Ling Jiou Mountain, which houses more than 100 nuns and monks today. He had begun traveling around the world to collect information and garner support for the Museum of World Religions as his contribution to interreligious dialogue and world peace. The vision of the Museum was born during the retreat. It opened in Taipei in

2001 after a ten-year preparatory period in which Shifu's followers in Taiwan contributed their generous efforts, both personal and financial, to make this gift to the world a reality. Since its opening, the Museum has served as a platform for religious education and interfaith dialogue both in Taiwan and internationally. I was fortunate to be involved in the last stages of the planning of the Museum and then to be invited to run its international interfaith program after its completion.

When the world was reeling in shock after the tragedy of September 11, 2001, Shifu immediately reached out to the Muslim world by initiating a series of Buddhist-Muslim dialogues, to foster understanding and cooperation between Buddhist and Muslim communities. This series of dialogues, which have been held in twelve countries so far, is just one example of the many international interfaith activities that the museum and its outreach organization, the Global Family of Love and Peace, a UN-affiliated non-governmental organization, are involved in.

When our sons Florian and Benjamin left home to start college a few years ago, I was finally able to join the nuns at the monastery in a three-week intense retreat guided by Shifu. The scroll in the hallway in front of my room, beautifully written in Shifu's own calligraphy, expresses the essence of his life and teaching in a nutshell: To go beyond the world is wisdom, to reenter the world is compassion. The early disciples who had followed Shifu to the mountaintop toward the end of his strict fasting retreat, imagining that they would become hermits just like Shifu, were in for a surprise when they were given the mission to establish the Museum of World Religions as part of their religious practice to benefit others. The Museum foundation is just one among various other foundations that were established to further the cause of education, charitable work, and disaster relief in Taiwan and abroad. Never forgetting his own experience as a war orphan and child soldier, with little chance of formal education during his early youth, Shifu founded an educational farm in the northern part of Myanmar to give other orphans the opportunity to study and establish a livelihood in organic farming.

Having himself experienced the reality of death at such a young age, Shifu also conducts the yearly solemn rituals and prayers of the "Water and Land Ceremony" in Taiwan, Hong Kong and Singapore, to help the departed and their families move on from suffering and find peace. This ceremony is attended by ten thousands of people every summer. In 2014, Shifu was given the highest Buddhist award by the president of Myanmar for his achievements.

While altruistic service born of boundless compassion is the essence of enlightened practice, that practice is sustained by times of retreat, meditation, and silence, times of "transcending the world." The practice of "transcending the world" can be as long as three years or more, and as short as one minute or even just one deep breath. Fully aware of the fact that those of us who have families to raise and jobs to maintain have little chance of going on retreat, Shifu has developed such methods as the One-Minute Meditation, which is now widely taught to school children in Taiwan to help them settle and focus, as well as to people in their busy jobs. Those who do find the opportunity to come to the short retreats for laypeople, which are regularly offered at the monastery, will be introduced to the Listening to Silence Meditation, which is the basic meditation method for laypeople and monastics alike and is described in Chapter 4 of this book. Since going through the basic steps of this guided meditation takes nine minutes, it is also called the Nine-Minute Meditation.

This modest book is meant as an introduction to Shifu and his teaching for those English-speaking students who attend retreats in Germany or at the international meditation centers established in Taiwan, Myanmar, Nepal, or the US. Of course it is also meant as a resource for general readers. The title is the translation of the name Hsin Tao—Hsin meaning the heart or mind, which is one word in Chinese, and Tao meaning the way. The book follows the basic structure of the Buddha's teaching of the Four Noble Truths, which briefly are summarized as follows:

1) Life is marked by dukkha—which is variously translated as "suffering" or "dissatisfactoriness"; 2) the root of dukkha lies in a dualistic view of self and other, which gives rise to the five poisons: delusion, greed, anger, pride and fear; 3) there is an end to dukkha, namely enlightenment or nirvāna; 4) the way of enlightenment is based on the practice of morality (sīla), meditation (samādhi) and wisdom (prajňā). This structure was the organizing principle behind my choice of Shifu's teachings, which I have translated from many different sources, which were kindly made available for me through the help of the nun Faang Shi for this book. Here is a very brief overview of the content of the individual chapters:

In Chapter One, Shifu tells his own life story, starting from his experiences losing his parents at young age and being drafted as a child soldier through his life-transforming encounter with Bodhisattva Guanyin, which made him dedicate his life to bringing relief to all who suffer. Shifu did not shy away from the intense suffering that he experienced during the time of strict ascetic practice in graveyards and the cave. Instead he pushed on all the way, almost to the point of death, and finally achieved a spiritual breakthrough that made him discover "that in our heart-nature which does not undergo the pain of life and death, that which is free from the suffering of saṃsāra (the round of rebirth)." All of Shifu's teaching is based on his enlightenment experience and his vow to help others discover that place beyond life and death as well, so that we can drop all fears and become our true, free and compassionate selves.

In Chapter Two, Shifu explains how the mistaken notion of a permanent Self and the selfish attitudes generated by it cause us to find ourselves in a world frayed by so many problems. Not clearly understanding where we come from and what we are, we engage in actions that are unskillful and harm both others and ourselves. But insight into the law of cause and effect, the truth of impermanence, and the truth of emptiness help give our life a new direction, teaching us not to waste it in the pursuit of fleeting things.

In Chapter Three, Shifu further elucidates the path of overcoming suffering by returning home to that central place and energy that each of us possesses, that place which is the core of the entire universe, namely nirvāna. To reach that place within us, it is helpful to start from taking our refuge in the Buddha, the teachings (dharma), and the community of practitioners (sangha) as the path to realizing our own enlightened nature. The precepts, meditation, and the wisdom teachings of the Heart Sutra helps us to systematically let go of everything that binds us and become free and compassionate like Bodhisattva Avalokiteśvara.

In Chapter Four, Shifu introduces the practice of Chan meditation as the most direct way to enlightening our hearts and minds and seeing our true nature. While there are different methods of practice in Chan, they all come back to stopping and seeing, namely stopping the distractions of our busy mind and seeing our original face, that which is most real in life. The most conducive way that Shifu has found to achieve the stilling of the heart and mind, necessary to reach the unifying state of deep meditative absorption (samādhi), is the Listening to Silence

Meditation, which consists of the four steps that are explained in this chapter. It is this form of guided meditation that Shifu uses to lead his students towards a deepening experience of samādhi, regardless of whether they have been practicing for decades in the monastery or whether they are beginners on the path.

The conclusion reminds us that the integration of Chan practice into our daily lives is that which counts the most, so that we may become persons of peace who deeply care for the well-being of all the members of our one Global Family. As Shifu always says: "When the heart is at peace, the world will be at peace."

Chapter 1

MY PATH THROUGH SUFFERING

I. A war-torn childhood

I was born in a small, remote village in the Northern part of Burma, now called Myanmar, in 1948. It was a time of war and upheaval which exposed me to the trauma of war from a very young age on. Burma had recently gained independence from the United Kingdom, and fighting and uprisings not only erupted in the border areas among different ethnic groups but also inside the country. The new government was under the constant attack of Communist rebels, and lawlessness reigned everywhere. Life was very difficult for ordinary people; they could not be sure at sunrise that they would still see the sunset. I was born into such an environment of conflict and strife, and from a young age I hated what the war did to people's lives—the violence, instability, and impermanence of it all. I often thought about how I could make the war simply disappear, and what it would take to have peace and harmony instead. This aversion to war and longing for peace became deeply ingrained in my whole being; it set the aspirations and goals for my future life.

The village in which I was born was called Lashio. The villagers, like my own family, were mainly farmers who grew opium among other crops like rice, wheat, or vegetables. But it was a mountainous region, and nothing really grew that well except for the opium. It was a very poor village. My own family was not of Burmese origin; they had come from the Chinese province of Yunnan many generations before my birth. Many people in our village were of Chinese origin like us; but there were other tribes too, all of us mixed together. My mother tended the fields, and my father worked as an ironsmith. One night when I was four years old, my mother looked at me lying in my bed, quietly shedding tears. I pretended to be asleep, but I instantly knew in my heart that my mother wanted to leave. I didn't dare to move, fearing that it would be too hard for her to do what she needed to. That night my mother left the house and walked away with my baby sister. I never saw her again. There was no news about her whereabouts whatsoever. I could not help but think that my mother did not want me any longer.

A few days later, I was out in the fields working with my father, harvesting rice. It was a good and plentiful harvest. We were on our way home when I saw many people coming towards us, a whole mountain full of people, grabbing my father and taking him away. "Where is my father going?" I thought. "What are all these people doing here—why are they grabbing him?" I ran after them as fast as I could, crying and screaming. I had no idea that this moment was very dangerous. I stood at a threshold of life and death; my young life could have ended right then and there. Some of the big people tried to stop me, to hold me down, but they could not. The only thought racing through my mind was "Where are they taking my father? I want to be with him. I want to see him." But it was useless, and from that day on I never saw my father again either.

After that I lived in my uncle's house as a small vagabond, roaming all over the neighborhood and countryside. My uncle had a small business selling cloth and medicine to the different tribes that lived in this remote part of Burma, and I would accompany him on his trips. In the very beginning, I keenly felt the anxiety of this kind of unsettled life and the pain of being separated from my mother, father, and sister. I did not understand the world one bit and wondered why all of this had happened to me, but gradually I got used to my new life at my uncle's house. He liked spicy food, which I could not swallow myself. Each meal became a kind of ordeal for me until I eventually got used to the spiciness. About a year after my arrival my aunt died and my uncle's business failed. Instead of selling cloth he just went around to help as a worker in the fields or as handyman, taking me along. I cried waiting for him while he was working. I cried when he returned. I just cried a lot in those days.

My uncle later remarried, and my step-aunt, who was kind, brought a small child with her into the marriage. All of this changed the dynamic between my uncle and me. Originally it had been just the two of us, but when he remarried he had to provide for all of us. His temper soured. When he was in a bad mood, he would scold or even beat me sometimes. One day when I was seven or eight years old I simply ran away and managed to find work herding cows for people from one of the tribes. Sometimes I would also watch their children. I really liked keeping the cows, out there in nature all by myself. But my uncle came looking for me and threatened the family I stayed with, telling them, "I'll chop you down if you don't return the boy to me." And so he brought me back home with him.

Not much later, when I was nine years old, someone convinced me to join the army so that I would get an education. I had seen other children from our village studying books or writing with a brush, and I thought it would be great fun to learn how to read and write. And so I agreed to go along. This is how I became a child soldier in a guerilla army. It was a great opportunity for me—here I was together with a whole group of people, walking from the northern tip of Burma to the south, crossing through forest, streams and rivers, high mountains and valleys. It was extremely dangerous; there were wild animals and poisonous snakes, and even a moment of carelessness might end your life. I was a rather small and skinny boy, and there was no horse to ride on. We had to keep on walking, walking, walking. My companions, seeing how young and weak I was, would take pity on me and sometimes carry me along on their backs until they got tired themselves. Then I had to walk again on my own until someone would pick me up again and carry me some more. We were surrounded by enemies who were hiding in the forest, but I did not understand what we were doing. Who were these enemies? What were we afraid of? What kind of danger were we facing? We rested during the day and only walked at night, under the cover of darkness, trying not to make any noise, our ears straining for the tiniest sound that might indicate danger. More than two months later, we eventually reached the southern tip of Burma on the border with Thailand. This is where they started to train me as a soldier, so that I could join the army for real.

My training period lasted three months. Since I was so small, there was no outfit that fit me. Everything was too big—my clothes, even my shoes—what a mess! Again I was bewildered, wondering what we were training for. Turning right, turning left, standing at attention, and saluting over and over again: what was it all for? It took some time before it dawned on me that we were training for war. A guerilla army means war, and we were learning how to kill people! And why would we learn this? We were told it was to protect our country. But which country were we protecting? The country, as it turned out, was Taiwan, a country far away across the ocean. We were training to recapture mainland China from the hands of the communists who had overtaken it in 1949.

I was a young and mischievous boy in the army, without any relatives to rely on for help or to take care of me. The bigger ones took advantage of the smaller boys who had to fend for themselves. We eventually learned how to behave towards the grown-ups, what to do and what not to do. There was a senior army officer who took care of me. Perhaps it was because of him that I never thought of running away. He made a small cot for me to sleep on, next to his own cot, and in the morning he helped me to wash my face and put on my uniform. He often corrected me, and this is how I learned to obey the rules and to respect others. Just as importantly I also learned how to love myself.

I also had some friends and playmates in the army. I remember one incident during that time when I wanted to play and ran off to visit my friend from a different unit. I didn't know that our unit was supposed to move on that day and that we were not allowed to spend the night. When I got back the next day, I was punished and locked up in a dark cave without any light for seven days. I could not see the slightest thing, and no matter how much I cried and screamed, nobody answered. This was where I experienced for the first time the horror of darkness, of being completely alone and helpless. All I had done was visit my friend, to spend one night there, and then I was locked up in a dark hole for so many days as punishment! I was totally bewildered; I did not understand anything about life, this random turn of events, or why this had to happen to me at all.

During my time in the army, I experienced war and death, the impermanence and fragility of life. I was ten years old when I saw an army deserter shot right in front of me. This experience created a lasting impression on me. It was so cruel. This man probably had tried to run away without much further thought because he was homesick.

One moment he was as alive as a rising dragon and a prancing tiger, and one bang later he lay dead on the ground, covered in blood. I saw all of the misery brought on by war and understood clearly that war is the origin of suffering. I had the thought of making the war cease and disappear. In the beginning I dreamed of becoming a revolutionary, and wage war to stop the war. But one look at history tells you that nobody has ever succeeded in this kind of endeavor before, and even if they did, conflict and war would break out again soon after their death. When I realized that this would be a pointless endeavor, I felt sad and depressed. Of course, our original goal of attacking and recapturing mainland China had not materialized, and so I returned with the remaining army to Taiwan when I was thirteen years old.

II. Encountering Bodhisattva Guanyin

After arriving in Taiwan in 1961, I started going to an army school to continue my education, still as a soldier. At that time I constantly thought about human life, its value, and how to give life meaning and worth. But I was also like the other youth around me, dreaming about chivalry, setting right what was wrong and ridding the world of every kind of injustice. I started practicing martial arts with my friends, and we read many martial arts novels.

Every time I finished a book I felt that I had lived an entire life. The world seemed like a chessboard to me, with people only bent on attacking and killing or on striving for fame and richness. I could see greed, anger, insolence and pride as the root of suffering, and keenly felt that human life was like a theater, that everything was impermanent.

When I was fifteen, I happened to be at the house of a medical doctor who told some stories about Bodhisattva Guanyin. He called her "Mother Guanyin," and at the very moment I heard the name my heart was so deeply moved that tears started flowing. I did not understand why I had this reaction—nothing had happened other than hearing the name. Reflecting on that moment later on I felt that I must have a deep karmic connection to Guanyin, and so I wanted to find out more about her—all the facts, texts, and stories related to her. This is how I initially encountered Buddhism. I grew up in a Buddhist country in a Buddhist environment, but if my parents were Buddhist, I would have been too young to know it, since I lost them so early. There were Christians and Muslims among the tribes to which I ventured with my uncle, but I was too young to understand anything. As I read the Universal Gate—the chapter on Guanyin in the Lotus Sutra and the legend of princess Miaoshan—I was inspired by Guanyin's compassionate vow before the Buddha not to enter nirvana before all beings had been saved from suffering. I learned that Guanyin can take many different forms to help people in need. She can solve all the situations of danger and distress that people might find themselves in, free them from all of their troubles, and heal them from all of their ailments. I felt that I wanted to learn from Guanyin's spirit of great compassion and self-sacrifice for others, and so I took her as my inspiration and idol. Like Guanyin, I wanted to bring relief to all those who suffer. To make myself firm in this intention, I tattooed my two arms with the following vows: "May I awaken to repay Guanyin's kindness" and "I will never rest until I attain Buddhahood."

My heart was so full of gratefulness to Guanyin. She was the one who made me feel protected and loved in this vagabond and unsteady life of mine in which I had to mostly rely on myself. She helped me when I felt low and lonely. I wanted to follow in her footsteps and take her great compassionate spirit of helping people as an example to follow life after life. This initial encounter with Guanyin started me on my path of learning about Buddhism and trying to see the world in the light of Buddhism. I became a vegetarian, which was a big challenge at my military school, where I was ridiculed by my classmates and teachers. I often had to go hungry, eating just a little rice and tofu without even a bit of soy sauce for seasoning.

There was a temple near my school where I began to drop by almost every day after classes. It was there at Chaoyin Temple that I first heard about Chan meditation, which I then slowly began to practice on my own.

III. Searching for the Path in Life

A round seventeen and eighteen years old, at the time when we undergo the greatest changes, I was still a seeker, constantly pondering the meaning of life and wondering what concretely to do with my own life. I was still in the army at the time, and I kept questioning whether this was something I wanted to continue doing. In the meanwhile, I had also started to venture out into other religions, such as Christianity. For a year or so I attended services at a church, listened to sermons and sang hymns. I also prayed, but all of it was more of an emotional approach. I did not really sit down to study the scriptures, since I did not have time for this. I also checked out Taoism a bit, but I think what really brought me back to Buddhism was an encounter I had with a former monk who had become a soldier in the army. He taught me how to recite the Great Compassion Mantra and the Heart Sutra, and introduced me to the basics of Buddhist thought. At school, we had studied the Confucian classics, which constituted the moral foundation of my life, but I steadily became more deeply immersed into the world and practice of Buddhism. As I contemplated the constant changes and impermanence of life, I slowly came to understand the nature of this world and what truth consists of. And so in the end I thought about becoming a Buddhist monk to accomplish the work of saving people, saving the world, and saving myself. If I could do this, I would live up to my ideal of love and peace. And so I decided to leave my school and quit the army.

I asked for a leave and simply did not come back on time. During my absence I kept myself busy. I set out into the ocean on a small bamboo raft from Pingtung, but as soon as I was out in the water, the waves threw it back onto the shore, and there was nothing much to do about it. Later I thought about traveling back to Burma and finding some work there, but that plan came to naught. At that point, returning to the army was no longer an option for me, and I figured that if I spent some time in prison it would invalidate my military status, and they would allow me to leave the army.

The judge in my case however had not intention of sentencing me and kept asking if I wanted to return to the army school to continue my education. He simply wanted to send me back to school. But when I told him clearly that

I had no such intention, that I wanted to leave the army, he sentenced me to more than one year in prison for deserting. That sentence was finally reduced to eight months.

The time in prison was a turning point for me. It was the hardest time in my life. I was not treated as an army deserter but as a criminal and a spy. The reasons for this were unclear to me, since I had been part of the army since I was a child. In any case, I was subjected to constant interrogations, three times a day or more. They would also call me in the middle of the night gleefully waking me up for the next interrogation. I was questioned over and over again: "Why did you really run away? Why would you take such a decision?" For about a month I was not allowed to receive any visitors in prison, but I did not really have any friends anyway. When all of the interrogations yielded no result, they finally sent me to the penal colony in Tungshi, Chiayi, where we had to build a new coastal defense facility. We worked ceaselessly during low tide. The wind blasted us with sand, which filled our eyes and noses and caked to our faces. We were only given a break from slugging along like this during the high tide. It was unbearable.

Prison was a dark hole; it was hell. If you had money or connections, you could have quite a good time there, but without any of those, you were out of luck. You could work hard at building up some social relationships, but if you were not good at it you would end up with beatings. This prison experience drove me more than ever to practice a spiritual path and become a Buddhist monk. In my heart I felt that I had not done anything bad—I had not attacked or robbed anyone—all I had wanted was to enter the order and lead a life of religious practice, working to save the world. As I dwelled on these kinds of reflections, I was no longer overwhelmed by the feeling that I was being treated unjustly. Rather, I felt that I should face my sentence and time in prison with inner peace. Finally my prison term came to an end, but then I found out that one needed a guarantor to leave prison. Where should I find such a person? It took some more time until a guarantor was found and I was finally released.

My first thought after leaving prison was to quickly find a temple where I could become a monk and take up my religious practice. This had been my goal all along. Even though I searched around, I could not find a temple that seemed right for me, and so I put the idea aside for the time being, telling myself that I should not be too much in a rush. My life in the army had been very sheltered; I had no experience of life in society, nor did I know much about it. I decided I should find some work to get a better understanding of real life in the world. I did every kind of job—as a cook on a ship, a toilet cleaner, a construction worker, an actor and a worker in a rice shop. When I applied for my first job as manual laborer in Tainan, I said to the boss "I am ready to start right after I eat something." "No", he said, "first you work, and then you eat." I was starving, and yet he insisted that I had to work first. How could he be so miserly? I thought this over and left that job on the second day.

Next I was a crew member on a ship. When I found this job in Kaohsiung, I was told that the ship would leave in 3 months. But when I arrived at the harbor at the appointed time, the departure was delayed for yet another month. While I was waiting for the ship to take off, I could only afford the cheapest food there was—dried noodles. When we finally boarded the ship, it turned out to be a small and slow fishing boat that was only suited for fishing close to the coast, not for navigating the deep sea. As soon as we took off into the high waters I became very seasick and kept vomiting so wretchedly that my organs were about to give out. I felt that this was it, that I was going to die. In this agony I remembered to take my recourse to Guanyin and repeated her holy name over and over again, until I forgot everything else and fell asleep. When I woke up again, I was fine.

My different experiences and difficulties at work taught me more about the hardships of life and its unpredictability and impermanence. They helped me to understand more clearly what causes suffering. They convinced me that we need to face life's constant changes and challenges with courage and faith and that we need to live fully and wholeheartedly.

This attitude revealed life's joyful side to me. At that time I did not have any family or relatives, nor even a single friend, but my wholeheartedness and courage soon brought me many. My positive attitude helped me adapt to my work environment and create a living space. I felt that each job and experience has something to teach us; it has its joys and limitations and its own space for thinking. We come into life as strangers, born into an unfamiliar environment. We slowly grope our way into life, face it, get used to it and eventually understand it. Through it all we interact with others and gradually establish a basis of cooperation.

After working at several different jobs, the day arrived when I felt that if I went down this road, I might not be able to fulfill my heart's desire to become a monk and save the world from suffering. My last job as a worker at a rice shop had been especially hard, since I had to lift very heavy bags of rice onto a bicycle and deliver them all throughout town. My body was so exhausted that my health started failing me, so I wanted to leave this environment behind before it was too late. I felt that this was the moment for me to enter a spiritual path that would bring more meaning and value to my life, one that would give it a clear-cut direction and goal.

IV. Becoming an Ascetic Practitioner

In 1973 I enrolled at the college of Foguang Shan Monastery in Kaohsiung. I passed the entrance exams, but I did not have money to pay the tuition fee. "Never mind," the admissions officer told me, "just become a monk and we will help you with everything." And so I decided to enter the monastic life and took my precepts very soon. The monk who conferred the precepts transmitted the Chan lineage to me, and this launched me into serious practice of meditation. I started to devote all of my time to sitting, so much so that I lost the taste for everything else, including attending classes, which seemed like a waste of time to me. Finally I left the monastery after a little more than one year of studies to embark on a path of ascetic practice in solitude.

My strong attraction to ascetic spiritual practice was inborn, and I had nurtured it all along by reading the accounts of accomplished Buddhist practitioners throughout the ages. One of my great models was Mahakāsyapa, the senior disciple of the Buddha, who was known for his severe ascetic practices. It was to him that the Buddha had passed on his teaching in a mind-to-mind transmission. I also took Milarepa, the great Tibetan Yogi, as one of my teachers. I was very eager to verify their teachings through my own practice. All of these great practitioners had achieved awakening through suffering; they had used suffering as a means of great spiritual accomplishment. Looking back on my own life from the time I was four years old until I entered the monastery, I realized that I had been in the midst of suffering all along! I had never dwelt on that aspect of suffering, because my experiences had taught me so many things—and there was also joy in that.

The reason why we engage in severe ascetic practice is that we are searching for the truth—we want to experience and testify to it. Ascetic practice involves training the body and mind; it is a way of growing and a process of experiencing. We set out from the keen awareness that this life is short and impermanent, full of suffering, and that we live it mostly in a state of confusion until it is suddenly over one day. So if we want to understand clearly what life is all about, even if we just want more clarity and meaning in our lives, then we have to practice well and be ready to endure some pain.

I began my life in solitude in an old house in the outskirts of Taipei where I stayed for three months. This was the first time for me to practice in seclusion, and it was very scary and lonely. I was sitting by myself, completely cut off from the outside world and so oblivious of anything happening there that I would not even have noticed if the sky had come down. I felt very restless at the time, overwhelmed by feelings of isolation and boundless loneliness which invaded me from all directions, especially in the long, dark nights. These initial experiences taught me that living apart from the rest of humanity is painful, that my own being is something painful too and that I had to learn how to subdue my own mind in order to cope. The practice of meditation is to constantly adjust our thoughts and feelings, to lead them into the right direction until we reach inner peace of mind. It took me about a year until I could really overcome my own feelings of loneliness.

In the meanwhile, I had I moved on to Yuanming temple in Ilan County in the Northeastern part of Taiwan. It was a shabby and very damp old temple, with a graveyard to the east and surrounded by forests on all sides. It is here that I began my austere practice of sitting at least eighteen hours a day in meditation. Also, I would only take one meal before noon, which consisted mostly of brown rice sprinkled with some sesame seeds. There were many difficulties that arose in this environment.

The greatest difficulty was that my body and mind would not listen to me. When I first started sitting in the Lotus posture, my legs would soon become unbearably sore and numb, as if pricked by pins and needles or burned by fire. At times, the pain in my whole body would become so intolerable that I would think, "Why should I make myself so miserable? Why not find an easier way to practice?" But when I would remember how the Buddha sat firmly in deep concentration (samādhi) until he achieved enlightenment, and I would regain my confidence and the determination to persist in my practice.

Attuning the mind to the practice is even more difficult than the adjustment of the body, since the mind is very difficult to steer when it becomes scattered. Sometimes I would become sluggish or impatient because of the physical discomfort of the body. At other times, I again desperately wished for some signs of human life to appear to alleviate the piercing loneliness of my heart. But as my body gradually adapted to the posture and my mind became more focused, I experienced the light, at-ease and egoless state of samādhi in meditation. This blissful state alleviated my fear of isolation and the pain in my heart.

My body was no longer distressed by the sitting, and my fear of isolation had subsided; but new troubles arose one after another in the form of illusory states of mind. When these negative mental states occur, one can no longer discriminate between reality and illusion. As a result, the energy of the whole body dissipates. It is just as if one had taken the wrong medicine. When these states arise, it is important to keep one's vigilance and mindfulness. This is why spiritual practice is likened to entering a battlefield. But when one practices in accordance with the right teaching, these negative states will be overcome.

I usually sat near the front door of the temple for meditation, but during the negative states, my meditation was soon disrupted by the noise of the door closing and opening or by banging on the door. When I got up to check out the situation, I did not see anyone, even though I felt that clearly some beings were drifting in and out of the temple. These disturbances caused by spirits continued for some time, until I moved away from the door and onto an old bed inside the room to continue my meditation in greater peace. But this bed happened to be over a snake pit. As I was meditating, they would hang on the posts and beams, hissing at me, or slither around my seat until they were tired and fell asleep. Some people advised me to block the snake pit or even kill the snakes, but I did not follow their advice. I felt that my encounter with the snakes was an opportunity for me to practice openheartedness and compassion for all beings. All sentient beings are naturally endowed with Buddha nature. If we treat them with loving kindness and compassion, their aggression and vicious nature will be removed. I felt that the snakes would not harm a spiritual practitioner, and since there was no enmity or hatred between us we did not bother each other.

Because of the dilapidation of Yuanming temple I finally moved on to Lingshan Pagoda in Gitsulun. It was also immersed in boundless loneliness, deprivation and silence. My meditation there was again disrupted by all kind of outside noises that sounded like gongs or people chattering or cannons or footsteps. However when I investigated, I never found anything. "Could the noises be an illusion brought on by my own deluded state?" I asked myself. I called out to Master Chaofan who was also staying there at the time. He confirmed hearing the same noises, saying, "I am enjoying listening to them."

One night, while I was sitting in meditation, a heart-wrenching sound of sobbing and weeping suddenly reached my ears. It went on for a long time and sounded as if someone was extremely distressed. My heart became agitated and my mind scattered, and I was unable to cope with it. I followed the sound down to the storage room where the ashes of the deceased were kept, but there was nothing there. As soon as I left and went back up to the second floor, the weeping started again. So I began to recite the Great Compassion Mantra, and the sound vanished before I had even finished my recitation. From then on I did not hear those eerie, gut-wrenching cries again.

Encountering the beings from the other world in this way did not scare me away. On the contrary, I found them to be helpful for my spiritual quest. They deepened my strong yearning for the Truth. I found that as long as I pursued my practice with diligence, even snakes, ghosts and spirits would be respectful.

After two years at Lingshan Pagoda I moved again and settled down at the Lungtan public cemetery near Ilan. When you practice in a graveyard, you really feel that human life is so evanescent and unreal. I saw how people carried the corpses up the hill to bury them and then returned back home. Sometimes the rotting corpses were scattered around among the graves, with birds and worms picking on them. Facing this cruel reality of human existence, life and death seemed to me like a dream. We think that life is such a big affair, but what is left of it in death? Both life and death are unreal. When I meditated on the impermanence of human life in the graveyard I slowly lost my own attachments and my fear of death. Up to this time, my heart would sometimes still be quite at unrest, with deeply ingrained cravings and desires for love sporadically popping up in it. I would counteract the intruders by contemplating the impermanence and painfulness of life in which nothing ever remains beautiful or lasts forever. This is especially true for the human heart, which is always changeable and quite treacherous. There is no everlasting sentiment or love. With that insight, my cravings and desires were cut through, and I sat with renewed determination to devote myself fully to my practice. I knew that I would not ever find a path in this world which is happier or more reliable than spiritual practice.

The goal of practice is always to subdue and pacify our heart and mind. Without practice, we generally do not have the ability to settle our mind. And without the ability to settle our mind, we cannot help save others from suffering.

We settle our mind through persistence in practice. This helps us to form our character and build up our power of endurance. Our compassion also arises out of endurance in practice. I have asked myself whether compassion is something inborn, or if it arises as a result of practice. I came to the conclusion that our ability to be compassionate is inborn, but that we need to form a habit of always nurturing a heart of compassion towards all beings. If we want to help others we also need wisdom. Wisdom is born out of solitude, out of silence.

I had already spent eight years mostly in solitude and silence, but I felt that my wisdom about life still needed to deepen and that my understanding was not yet sufficient. So I embarked on an even stricter ascetic practice of two years of strict fasting in a cave on Ling Jiou Mountain near Fulong, on the northeast coast of Taiwan. This is where our present monastery is located. The cave was also damp, and it was home to a snake which slithered around my meditation seat but never interfered with my practice.

Fasting helps us to deepen our practice, by proceeding from a coarse state of mind to a very clear and refined one. Abstaining from food supports this process of investigation and purification which involves the whole body. As we keep going, our mind becomes more and more dispassionate and quiet, which allows for deeper insights into the great matter of life and death. If we keep going, we eventually reach the point of a complete break-through.

During my fasting in the cave I only drank water and ate nine pills of "Baihuawan," a Chinese herbal medicine consisting of a hundred kinds of flowers (baihua), which are carefully chosen and prepared under the constant recitation of mantras. Taking nine pills every day just barely helps you to physically survive. Following this method I lost so much weight that I was reduced to skin and bones. When I meditated my bones directly touched the ground, and sitting, standing, walking and lying down became equally painful. I was in constant pain because all bodily tissue that cushions the nerves from direct touch had shrunk away.

As I was struggling with this physical pain, I kept asking myself, "Is there anything in all of this which is not in pain?" It is strange, but that which knew that the body is in pain, that itself seemed to be just fine. That which knows the pain, knows of no pain! This is how it gradually dawned on me that there is something deep within ourselves which does not suffer, even if we are half-dead from pain. This taught me to not focus my attention on the pain or mind it at all, but to instead pay attention to that inside which knows of no pain and can never be destroyed, no matter what. And so I discovered that in our heart-nature which does not undergo the pain of life and death, that which is free from the suffering of saṃsāra.

I thought of how many people are scared of life because they don't know where life comes from, and how many more are terrified of death, because they don't know where they'll go after they die; I remembered my vow before Bodhisattva Guanyin to devote my whole life to her out of gratitude and not to rest until I attain Buddhahood. I was thirty-six years old, and the time had come for me to fulfill this vow of compassion by coming back to the world to start my work of teaching and helping others.

Chapter 2

OUR HUMAN CONDITION: THE ROOTS OF SUFFERING

Why are we born into this world? And what is the purpose of our life? Do you know the answer to these questions? Perhaps we don't know why we were born or the reason why we are here. We are already here, so we simply keep going. But we don't want to simply keep going, we want to keep going well. We want a good life. Not only do we want a good life, we want a better life than the person next door. And that is still not quite enough—we want to outdo everybody else. This means we constantly attempt to climb higher. Trying to keep going and figuring out how to do this best becomes our life-long preoccupation.

We feel that we have to protect ourselves first and foremost, even at the expense of others. To protect ourselves and live a bit better, we need to make a bit more money. When our attempts to preserve ourselves become overly self-serving, we start hurting others. We begin to file people into categories: those we like and those we don't, those who are on our side and those who are against us. "If you help me, I will help you," we say. "But if you destroy me, I will destroy you." We trap ourselves into courting favors and causing grievances. In order to survive and to keep going, we feel that we have no other choice than to get ahead of others, even if it means taking advantage of them and leaving them behind. We defend our actions by claiming that the whole process is just about making a decent living for ourselves.

For some people, making a living is not just a matter of being able to eat every day, but about accumulating more and more money and putting it into the bank. For them, the meaning of life lies in their successful business and the profit they can make—the more the better. They believe that success will make them happy and content. If it was just a matter of being able to eat every day, perhaps there would not be such a big problem, but greed is another matter. Our greed, our insatiable desire for more, leads to constant tension between people, to fierce competition between companies and corporations, and ultimately to wars between countries. This greed is not just about our daily bread, but about the many extra things that we want, and so it becomes a destructive force that touches everybody and everything.

The truth is that our desires keep us constantly busy and on the run. The more desires we have, the more we need to work hard to fulfill them. But they seem to never stop—they constantly multiply. I want a good job, I want to enjoy myself, I want a romantic relationship, I want a husband or wife, I want children, I want to become influential and famous—the list is long and stretches us in all directions. The problem is that there is only one me and so many things I want—what can I do about it? No wonder that we often feel so tired and exhausted. We spend our lives in constant pursuit of things that ultimately are impermanent. And so we suffer, even though we might not notice it at first, since we are so used to going all the time.

I. The Five Poisons

Desire or greed is one of the three basic poisons that the Buddha taught as the origin—literally the accumulation of suffering. The other two are anger and delusion. Why are they called the "accumulation" of suffering? The reason for this is that much of the pain and frustration we may experience in our present lives has its origin in countless previous lives. In the course of those lives we have each created our own habitual tendencies. These habits are different from those of other people since both our individual and collective memories differ; they have been "accumulated" over a very long time of interacting with others. These different accumulated memories and tendencies are the origin of suffering.

When we speak of time, we speak of the past, the present and the future. These are called the "three worlds." Our time includes not only this present life, but countless lives in the past and countless lives in the future. All things in the world of phenomena are a matter of time; all life is a matter of time; everything is a matter of time. Yet time is impermanent.

Our constant interaction with others, both in past lives and this present life, creates our habitual tendencies. For example, some people are addicted to drinking alcohol, smoking cigarettes or taking drugs while others cannot get away from stealing. There was a child of a very wealthy company boss in Taiwan who was addicted to stealing. There was nothing that the parents could do about their child's compulsion: even giving him money did not make any difference. Whenever the child saw something he liked, he would just steal it. This went on until the child turned seventeen and very slowly started to change. It was a matter of time and acquired habit, and it was not easy to overcome once and for all.

Our difficulties and pain in life come from our way of thinking. When our way of thinking is dualistic, it creates antagonistic relationships with others which are fraught with pain. When our desires and greed cause grievances in others, what will be remembered is this kind of relationship. Greed leads to anger, which is the second poison. And since anger is an expression of a conflicted relationship, it means suffering.

The third poison in addition to greed and anger is delusion or confusion. Delusion is often the result of being confused about something, and confusion leads us to having very conflicted feelings about a certain matter. We are confused about many things, and our confusion makes us frustrated. When we don't understand a certain policy advocated by our government, we get upset and ask, "Why did they decide such a thing?" But if we get the full picture, we might even agree with the government's decision and no longer feel upset and frustrated. We become confused when we don't have the correct understanding of reality. In this mix of confusion, greed and anger we destroy the harmonious relations with others in our environment. We accumulate and spread all that which blocks and ruins life, and we don't have to wait long until we feel the pain caused by this destructive behaviour.

It is just like with the cells in our body – when they go against us, the result is a cancerous growth. But if the cells are well inclined towards us, we will be healthy.

Everything in life is ultimately a matter of memory. This means that my relationship to others and their relationship to each other is a function of our respective memories. This collective body of memory is the origin of suffering. When this body of memory creates friction between us, causing us to harm others and ourselves, the result is pain.

So the three poisons are desire or greed, anger and delusion. Greed is behind our likes and dislikes, which in turn causes us and others many grievances. You know how easily love can turn into hate. This happens all the time. When we don't get what we want we start envying those who have what we want. If we cannot get over our envy it transmutes into anger and hate. Out of anger and hate we do many misguided things and become confused. Anger, hate and confusion are forces so strong that they lead us into conflicts which explode into war.

Delusion is related to pride, which is an additional poison. When we feel that we are not respected by others and harbor thoughts such as, "you don't respect me, therefore I don't respect you," we set ourselves up for another conflict-ridden relationship. Add to this mix fear as yet another poison. When you look at another person and think, "I don't like the face of this guy. He looks like a jerk," your fear creates yet another antagonistic relationship with unwholesome consequences.

Greed, anger, delusion, fear and pride are the ingredients of our daily lives. They are the glue that binds us to each other, the debt that we incur. Without them, we might not have anything to do with each other. When we are given over to these emotions—I want you, I hate you, I fear you, I don't respect you—we put something in motion. What we put in motion is the force of Karma, which pulls us towards each other and propels us into the cycles of rebirth.

When we become parents, we have great hopes for our children, and expect much of them. But then we find out that it is not easy to make them fulfill our heart's desires. Why is that? We are bound together in this life by this mix of desire, anger, delusion, fear and pride. When we open the newspaper, we come across all these articles about people killing each other: children killing their own parents, husbands killing their wives, wives killing their husbands. Those are the kinds of stories that newspapers most like to print. Why is that so? If the news were not exciting enough, nobody would buy the paper and they would make no money. But when we have read those kinds of things long enough there eventually comes the day when we are no longer interested in them and stop buying the paper.

It is the same with the five poisons. They are the stuff that brings us together, the mutual debt that we incur and then have to pay back, but once we don't have any use for those poisons anymore, we will no longer produce those kinds of relationships. This is why we should not exaggerate our demands on our children or parents or other people. Instead, we should see everything in a much wider perspective. All things in our relations are in flux; nothing is guaranteed. If we want to insist on some kind of guarantee, or on a certain way things have to be, we end up frustrated and angry.

Where do we produce and store the five poisons? It is of course in our own heart and mind. The mind is called the origin of all evil. Why is that so? It is obvious—the mind is that which creates notions such as me, you, other people, and the rest of the world and then starts making distinctions between all of these. This leads to comparing, bickering, arguing, enmity—in short, to suffering, which is what we really mean when we talk about evil. Our mind is the origin of it all, since it grasps for things and gets attached to them as long as it has no clue about the truth of emptiness.

Do we know where our body comes from? It comes from our desires and our attachment to life. The body in reality is nothing but a product of karmic circumstances, something just like duckweed. The duckweed floats on the water and follows wherever the currents take it, forming a cluster with other duckweeds. When the wind blows, these clusters all drift apart and keep on floating until they eventually form new clusters. It is just like that with our body—it comes into existence because of karmic circumstances, and then disintegrates when those circumstances change. If we have done a lot of good in previous existences, we are born with a healthy, good body and live under fortunate circumstances. This is not the case if we have done a lot of bad in previous lives. Then we receive the results and our body suffers. But when we encounter the teachings of Buddhism, we are taught to let go of the notions of good and evil, to clear up all karmic residues and to be free in all circumstances—no matter whether good or bad. This puts our heart to rest and sets it free.

II. **Impermanence**

As we build our lives on the busy pursuit of things, there may eventually come a time when we realize that those things we have worked for so hard for are slipping through our fingers, that nothing is reliable. Perhaps this will be the first time that we get a sense of impermanence. Yet impermanence is the mark of everything that exists, without any exception. Impermanence—the fact that we cannot hold on to anything indefinitely—makes us suffer, even more so if we expect to be untouched by it. When we ignore impermanence we keep up our delusions, which propel us through this life and the painful cycles of rebirth. It is for this reason that the Buddha has taught the truth of impermanence as a cause of suffering. Once we are no longer deluded about impermanence, once we understand life in the light of impermanence, we can become free from the suffering caused by it.

Impermanence is the very first lesson we need to clearly understand as practitioners of the way. Everything in this world is impermanent—every life, every feeling, every possession, every relationship between people. Everything changes; nothing ever stays the same.

Everything comes into existence and perishes again based on karmic circumstances.

This world is impermanent. Perhaps we think that the universe is eternal, but that is not so. One day the universe will perish and everything in it will be gone. Just think of the great heroes from ancient history — the beautiful courtesans or the famous emperors. Where are they today? All of them, without exception have become empty ghosts. They had their chance in the past to make their appearance, but that time is over today. Now it is our turn to make a brief appearance on the stage of history.

Do you feel attached to this world? Or do you harbor a grudge against it? This world, no matter how much you love it, or how much you hate it, is impermanent. If we look at Chinese history, we see how each new dynasty has replaced the one that came before it up to the time of the Chinese Republic. The change of dynasties is like flowing water that never stays the same. It is still like that today. Our leaders and politicians come and go with their own ambitions and plans. Some really love their country and want to give everything for it; others don't care about their country and are caught up in their own constant struggles for power.

If we feel discouraged at times we have to remember that a government is in place for perhaps three or five years before a new government replaces the old one. Some governing cycles are longer, some are shorter. If we look around the world we can see how short-lived things are. Some countries have only been in existence a hundred or perhaps fifty years, which is not a long time. Governments rise and fall, leaders come and go, political ideas and attitudes change to adapt to the exigencies of the present time. Just as we cannot take a hold of the past to make it work in the present we also cannot take the present to apply it back to the past. There is no guarantee that our own country Taiwan will exist forever. It is so fragile. We simply cannot bank on anything.

This is also true for the Four Elements that make up all existence, including our own. Those elements are earth, water, fire and wind. They compose our body. When those four elements are out of balance, our heart gets embroiled in all kinds of passions and our body becomes sick. Now ask yourself if we are in control of the four elements. If we were, we would be able to stop our body from changing and getting old. We would not allow it to die. But of course, none of this is under our control. We don't know when we are going to die. We cannot be sure that we will die from old age one day. When the karmic circumstances that keep the four elements together like a cluster of duckweed change, the elements will disperse and the body will die. Some die very young—as embryos in the womb, as newborns, as toddlers or as young children. Others live up to a ripe old age, all depending on karmic circumstances that we are not in control of. Thus, the four elements cause us suffering. Therefore we are taught as Buddhist practitioners to contemplate the four elements and to clearly understand that they are unreliable and impermanent; they are empty of Self. This contemplation helps us to become be free of the suffering caused by the four elements.

In the Heart Sutra, the four elements are referred to as form or matter (rūpa). This includes both the physical world and the body with its organs. The sutra says "Form is not other than emptiness, emptiness is no other than form. Form is precisely emptiness, and emptiness is precisely form. Sensation, thought, impulse and consciousness are also like this." These five—bodily form, sensation, thought, impulse and consciousness are called the Five Aggregates (skandhas). Form (rūpa) means all visible phenomena, and sensation (vendañā) means everything that we feel. Thought (samjña) is what happens next in the process after our heart and mind have seen outer objects and developed feelings about them. The feelings and thoughts produce an impulse (samskāra), leading to action. Consciousness (vijñāna) means discrimination. Where does this discrimination come from? It is simple: we see things which trigger a reaction in our heart and mind, and that reaction leads us to discriminate between those things. The five aggregates together form our body and mind. In fact they would not exist without our discriminating consciousness. This is why the Heart Sutra tells us to look at them as empty. If they are empty, there is no Self! And if there is no Self, there is no body, no sensation, no thought, no impulse and no consciousness! In other words, there is no such thing as all of the constant changes and suffering.

The truth is that all of these changes which lead us to suffer are empty and unreal. They are produced through unreal phenomena in our heart and mind. Our own heart that clings to empty things is the culprit. The outward forms of evil and suffering are sins and calamities. If we can look at things this way, we gradually become free from the cycle of birth and death. Therefore keep contemplating things in this way: all the problems of this world are impermanent. All the countries of this world are unstable and will not be here forever. The four elements are empty and fraught with pain. No one is really in control of the five aggregates that appear as the Self. They change without ceasing. There is no such thing as the existence of an I. The existence of an I is nothing but a notion that we hold on to. If we don't hold on to the notion, which I is there? Therefore let us not be greedy for such a thing as an I; let us not cling to it.

It is the same with our desires. Let us not produce too many or hold on to them. The heart is like a tank swarming with lots of fish, both big and small. How could it not be stressed? When we have big desires causing lots of troubles, we are raising big fish in our tanks. When our troubles are small, the fish are small. When our heart's desires are very few, our life becomes spacious and happy. And when we speak of the cycle of birth and death, what do we really refer to? Where is it happening? It is happening right here in our fish tank heart. It is there that we give birth and death to all kinds of discriminating thoughts, because we are not yet familiar with the teaching of emptiness. And these thoughts keep changing with the speed of lightning. We can have ninety fleeting thoughts in the span of one moment—this is how quickly they chase each other. Everything that we see in the outside world is created by our thoughts. And since our thoughts keep changing so quickly, the things in the phenomenal world also change accordingly. They keep changing, changing until nothing is left. And when nothing is left, its starts again. When we chase after our impermanent thoughts and the changing things in the phenomenal world, when we grasp for them and become bound up with them, we are subject to coming and going, appearing and disappearing, birth and death. If we want to cut out all the troubles and dissatisfactions that are intrinsic to this, we have to stop the chasing thoughts in our heart and mind, the constant appearing and disappearing of fleeting thoughts and desires. Even when we think, "this world is so beautiful!" or "this world is so terrible," we produce that which is called birth and death, namely, impermanence. All of our dualistic notions are nothing but birth and death.

But how do we go about giving up our desires? It is by contemplating the teaching of the Heart Sutra, which tells us that "form is no other than emptiness." This means that we learn to see all things of the phenomenal world as no-things. If we can look at everything that happens, good and bad, what we like and what we don't like, as unreal, empty, without basis, and out of our control, we can gradually let go and be at peace with whatever happens to us. When we have few desires, we are no longer kept so busy in trying to fulfill them. Our heart and mind stop being engaged in constant activity and calm down. If we want our body and mind to be free, we simply need to let go of the world of things.

III. Karmic memory

Now let us come back to our initial question: Why are we born into this world? This answer lies in our past karma—which means life after life in the past leading up to this present birth. We know that life is created through the coming together of sperm and egg. So when we ask again where we come from, the answer is simple: from sperm and egg. Yet we all know that in this day and age we do not even have to use sperm and egg anymore to create life; we can clone animals, and could probably also clone human beings. And what do we need to do this? Just a single cell of the body! The fact is that each cell of the body contains information that can be decoded. We know this for a fact through DNA research. That stored up information, the DNA, is a memory. Our physical bodies store up our life memories. Each of our bodies is a memory matrix.

Everything in this world is a similar body of stored up memory. Our own body came into existence through the push and pull of karma. It is desire which made us enter into the realm of physical attraction, and when sperm and egg came together, our body slowly started to form. Our head developed eyes, ears, nose, and tongue, equipping us with the senses of sight, sound, smell and taste. Our body developed the sense of touch, and our mind the inner sense of discerning objects. These are the Six Senses that we speak of in Buddhism. They form our body of karmic memory. Every cell in our body is equipped with a different memory, and our present physical body is an accumulation of those memories.

So what do we mean by the cycle of birth and death? It means simply the change from one body of karmic memory into the next one. When we die, the present body is no longer there. And so we go and look for a new body to replace the old one. It is an exchange. But where do we go for the exchange? We go into the memory storage. You might think that our DNA is something alive that will no longer function after we die, but have we not passed it on to our progeny—our children and grandchildren? When we die, we change into a new body of karmic memory that is related to our previous life. Every place is full of memory, full of feeling, full of past grievances and hurts. Death does not mean that there is nothing there at all anymore. It just means that I am changing one piece of old hardware into a new one and moving on.

But let us ask once again—what is the cycle of birth and death? Perhaps we have formed some idea about it in our head by now, but do we really get it? Every single minute, the cells of our body are participating in that cycle of birth and death. Our metabolism is that cycle; every thought in our mind that comes up and disappears again is that cycle. The cycle never stops but moves on like a wheel. Even if we think that we are gone with death it still keeps turning. As long as we don't know how to become enlightened, our life keeps turning like a wheel that is propelled by the force of karma. Karma is nothing other than memory.

What we call the force of karma are our memories; the entire memories of one life from birth to death. And where do these memories come from? They come from a previous life. All circumstances in our present life—good luck and bad luck, good friends and bad friends, success and failure in our work or business, the changes that we go through, our relationships, our parents, our marriage partners, and our children—all of this is a memory from the past. There are good memories and bad memories, and everything that life presents us with now is based on those memories. This means that in our present life we work out our past memories and, at the same time, create a new record of memories for our future life. This record then becomes the basis, the DNA, for our future life.

To understand the teaching on karma is very important in Buddhism. Not only do we need to understand it, but we need to believe that every cause has an effect. Karma is the DNA of our life. If our interactions create a positive karma, we can live a good life. But if the opposite is true, we end up hurting and killing each other.

Nowadays we grow up studying many things here and there and are exposed to many different thoughts and ideas, so we may not be so convinced that the teaching of karma is true and applies to everything. But if we understand the function of memory, of cause and effect, then our life is built on a clear structure and we know how to proceed. If we are confused about the function of memory, there is no clear structure to our lives.

When something bad happens to us—when for example our fortunes turn and we suddenly fall from richness into poverty, or when someone does something to hurt us, we may get very upset and vengeful. "Why did this happen to me?" we ask. "Why did he do this?" In our suffering and confusion we are not able to think straight and might well do something that we later regret. But if we can stop in our tracks and remember that the karmic connections which we have established in a past life are the origin of everything that happens to us in this life, then we will not give in to those feelings of ill-will and revenge. If we are given opportunities in this present life to earn a good living, it is because we have we helped others in the past and been generous. This is the fruit that we reap. But if there is nothing that we are reaping right now, if we are poor, we can make an extra effort. What is important is the right attitude of our heart, body, and mind. If we are full of good intentions, if we are willing to serve rather than being served, and if we are able to persist, then our fortunes will slowly turn again. If we have serve others, and if we share some of our wealth when we are in a position to do so, we create positive memories for others and ourselves, and we build up a treasure for our present and future lives.

As long as we are not yet familiar with Buddhist teachings, our lives dance to the tune of our past memories. They rise and fall like the music—now high and now low, now fast and now slow. If we have no plan, no goal and no principles, we live lives that tend to be rather complicated and confused. Our confusion is enacted by our body, mouth, and mind. Our body is just fine as long as there is not a something there that leads it on. The body in itself is not complicated or confused at all. But once it has been led on by something, it commits acts of lust, gluttony, stealing and killing. And how about our mouth? When we get into an argument with somebody else, it is always voiced with our mouth. Who does not know this from marital disputes? If we do not keep our mouth under control, if we insist that we are right, our disputes can become violent. A dispute often starts from an opinion which builds up to pit one camp against another camp. When we call each other male chauvinists or feminists for example we set up such a camp.

Our mouth, like our body, also relies on something else before it springs into action. By itself, the mouth is not the problem. The problem is the mind. When our mind is harboring the fivenpoisons—greed, ill-will, confusion, fear and pride—we use our mouth to express them and our body to act them out. And then we don't correct the greatest culprit, our mind, but only punish our mouth and body. But if we can transform our mind and rid it of greed, ill-will and confusion, our mouth and body will also be become pure. And if our mind, body, and mouth are purified, the structure of our life, will also become very expansive and pure. And with that, we will live at peace.

IV. The Six Realms

We need to be very clear about the fact that the mind is the origin of all things. It is the mind that creates our karmic body of memory and propels us into the cycle of birth and death. Life is constantly in motion, flowing just like water, rising and falling like the waves—high and low, high and low, birth and death, life and death.... Life takes on different forms as it flows—in this wave I might be born as a woman, in the next wave I might be born as a man, and in the wave after that I might even be born as a mouse. Every life is equal; the only difference is that, depending on my actions, my present life might be endowed with greater or lesser blessings. If there are many blessings, if we have generated a lot of good karma, our present life will be good, strong and healthy. If our blessings are small, if we have generated a karma that is marked by the three poisons, our present life will be more difficult and we will not have as much capacity to enjoy it, since it might take on a physical form that is very small and weak.

Every single life in this world is created by our consciousness, which is informed by our interactions with others. We could call our mutual relations in life interactive karma. This interactive karma creates the six realms of rebirth, which are spoken about in the Buddhist scriptures. We experience different degrees of suffering in all of them, no matter whether they are the three "good" realms or the three "bad" realms.

The first is the realm of the heavenly beings. We reach that realm if we have been very altruistic in life and done many good things. But even though we enjoy ourselves in heaven, we are still not exempt from impermanence.

Heavenly beings will also eventually get old and die all alone when their good karma and lifespan come to an end. The second realm is that of human beings. Our lives as human beings turn around such notions as there is and there is not, yes and no, good and bad, me myself and all others, and the desire for fame and fortune. All of this makes us suffer. We are born, become sick, get old and die, struggling all along to achieve some measure of fortune and recognition. The third realm is that of the titans. These are beings who are jealous of other people's good fortune and think of nothing all day long but competing and fighting with others. Because of their aggressiveness, jealousy, hot excitability and garrulousness, the titans suffer —even though their realm is still considered one of the good ones. So even though the realms of the heavenly beings, the titans and human beings are called the three good realms, they are still fraught with dissatisfaction and pain.

If it is already like this with the "good" realms of rebirth, what can be said about the "bad" ones? The first one of those is the realm of the animals, which is created by an attitude that is devoid of any reason and completely given over to the three poisons—desire, ill-will and delusion. The animals lead an existence of slavery and fear. For example, we raise animals such as cows, horses, pigs, chicken, geese and fish that we will eventually kill in order to eat them. The realm of the animals is one in which the stronger ones eat the weaker ones, who live in constant deep fear that their lives will be snatched away from them. The second bad realm is that of the hungry ghosts. The realm of the hungry ghosts is created by greed, passion, stinginess and a complete lack of compassion for others. The greed and desires are burning like a fire, and that is why the hungry ghosts experience constant thirst and hunger. Finally there is the realm of the hell beings. It is created by a murderous heart that feels nothing but disgust at everything. Since nothing at all goes according to its will, it never feels the slightest joy or inclination to do good. This is why it is stuck in the place of deepest suffering. If the denizens of hell manage to escape, they experience the suffering of the borderland, which is one of a very quick succession of birth and death, birth and death. This means that as soon as they are born, they die again, and then they come back to life only to quickly die again. If hell beings manage to be reborn as animals for example, their lives as animals are extremely short lived.

This gives us a basic idea of the six realms of rebirth. They are created by the attitudes in our heart and mind. They exist in the psychic as well as in the physical realm. Whenever we make our hearts into revengeful and murderous pits, we create hell both for ourselves and others. No one who thinks about all of the violence, the conflicts and wars that continue to ravage the earth would have the slightest doubt about this fact.

It is extremely rare to be born as a human being, and this is why it is so important not to waste this life in the pursuit of impermanent things. Only human beings can fully awaken and realize their true self. Even though we are pulled into the constant cycle of birth and death through our desires and attachments, we are equipped with reason and a conscience that tell us to do what is wholesome and avoid what is evil. But forces that pull us into the wrong direction are often very strong. The experience of suffering and the recourse to the teaching of the Buddha help us to uncover the wisdom of letting go, the wisdom of emptiness. Our lives in this body of karmic memory are so much dictated by fear—the fear of not being loved; the fear of being alone; the fear of not achieving what we want; the fear of getting ill, turning old and dying; the fear of being separated from loved ones; the fear losing our families, homes or country; the fear of being persecuted, harmed, robbed, or killed. All of those fears make us miserable. We become wary of this world in which people don't get along, in which they persecute and harm each other in such violent and destructive ways. We want out get out this sort of hell, out of this cycle of birth and death in which people inflict so much suffering on each other. The way to do this is to learn from Buddhism how to free ourselves from birth and death. Then when we come back again, we are no longer afraid, no matter where we are. Even if we were thrown into a frying pan we would not fear. But when we have not yet overcome birth and death, the wheel continues on and on—you fry me, and I fry you in return; you hate me and I hate you in return. It is so tiring!

Rather than continue to create this kind painful karmic memory we want to transform and purify it. How do we do this? We do this by understanding that the things of the phenomenal world outside give rise to our attachments, and that our thoughts cause us internal blockages. The Buddha is telling us that we need to look at both the things in the phenomenal world and the sensations they trigger in our heart and mind as unreal. Our thoughts and emotions are also just fleeting phenomena without any real basis of existence. They are nothing but illusions. There is no need to hold on to them. If you can look at things in this way, it will help you to no longer grasp for them and become entangled in them. If we grasp for things, we become entangled in the pain of dualistic thinking.

It is just like with a camera or a tape recorder. The images or sounds on the outside are recorded on the inside, and this recording is of a composite nature—impressions from outside and reactions from the inside. All of our thoughts are of this composite, constantly changing nature. Is there an I to be found in any of this?

How then do we transform and purify our body of karmic memory? How do we become free from the cycle of birth and death? How do we leave behind the suffering of the six realms of rebirth? How do we establish a plan and purpose for our life? The answer is simply this: Take your refuge in the Buddha, his teaching and his community of disciples, and enter the path of the bodhisattva. Make a vow and give rise to a heart of great compassion. Ask yourself what it is that you can do for other living beings. Start out from keeping the precepts, cultivating concentration (samādhi) and wisdom. The precepts, samādhi and wisdom help us to liberate the six realms of existence that we create in our own hearts and minds. The power that dissolves the three poisons and all the seeds which create the suffering of the six realms is the power of great compassion. A heart of great compassion which is nurtured by the precepts, samādhi and wisdom transforms our consciousness and destroys the gates of hell. Does it seem difficult? Do not worry about it but start slowly; all the buddhas and bodhisattvas are helping you.

Chapter 3

OVERCOMING SUFFERING

We sentient beings are consigned to endlessly circling the six realms and often feel the pressure and fear caused by this life in samsāra, the cycle of birth and death. This was what I came to realize early on in my life. Otherwise, why would I have started my strict ascetic practice? When I began my life of seclusion and solitude in that dilapidated pagoda, the question I wanted to resolve was first of all that of my own self. What was my central problem? It was the problem of birth and death. This included the problems of sexual desire; suffering; and the fear of sickness, old age, loneliness and death itself—all these problems that kept popping up inside of me.

So what is it that we look for when we take up Buddhist practice? We are mainly concerned with looking for a way to end our troubles, to overcome suffering, and then based on that, to go and help others do the same. To be able to do so, we have to start from a serious inquiry, earnestly asking ourselves: where do my troubles and problems really come from? Do they not stem from my entanglements in so many things that are conditioned by my karma? We hold on to everything—good karma and bad karma, and once we hold on to something we become entangled in it. And that is the beginning and cause of all our woes.

A life in seclusion then is a way to cut off the entanglements caused by things from the outside, not allowing them to become new problems, and to take care of the problems that are already there inside of us. In other words, taking on this kind of life solves the problem of your own self.

There are many great masters who were very diligent in their practice of asceticism, dwelling in the depths of a forest or wilderness, in mountain caves or on graveyards. They used very strict and painful methods to arrive at the realization of truth, to cut off all attachments and troubles, leaving behind all notions of good and bad. In this way they were able to really enjoy complete freedom and peace of heart and mind.

My own aspiration was not different from theirs. How could I cut of the trail of my problems and overcome the cycle of birth and death? And so I took those great masters as my spiritual guides and followed their example by retiring to an old dilapidated house, then to the graveyard and finally to a mountain cave to practice Chan meditation, to engage in quiet contemplation, and to realize the true essential nature that all of us possess as the Buddha taught us.

As long as we do not know our true essential nature, namely the truth of our spiritual self, we continue to circle around in the six realms, caught in our problems and worries, without finding a way out. When I was practicing in the cave, I constantly endeavored to arrive at a clear understanding, and when I started fasting, I concentrated my whole being on breathing. I felt that if I missed taking the next breath, I would die.

When we fast in this extreme way, we lose all of our strength, and death can happen at any moment. When we come to realize that death can happen at any moment, we really understand the impermanence of this life, and start to get in touch with our true essential nature—that which everyone of us possesses, at this very moment—that true innate knowledge which is resonating with these words I am saying. All of us possess this true innate knowledge, but we simply have not yet attempted to fully actualize it. And so we keep falling into our problems, into our life in samsāra, into all kinds of traps and fetters that we set up for ourselves, traps such as desire, anger and delusion. When I was fasting in the cave, I came to clearly realize that the true innate knowledge that all of us possess without any exception is our enlightened nature, that which is beyond life and death.

But let us return again to our query: How can we overcome suffering and put an end to our troubles? How can we be free of life in samsāra?

I.   Taking refuge in the Three Treasures

As Buddhist practitioners, we set out by taking our refuge in the Three Treasures—Buddha, dharma and sangha. The Buddha here refers to Buddha Śākyamuni. What does it mean to say that we take our refuge in Buddha Śākyamuni? Buddha Śākyamuni is someone who was not confused about anything, not about the universe and not about human life. He is the Awakened One, the one who has overcome all suffering and realized perfect wisdom. When we say that we take our refuge in the Buddha, it means that we want to study and learn from the Buddha, that we take our refuge in awakening. Buddha simply means awakening.

The dharma is what the Buddha taught. The Buddha already moved on, but he left us his teaching, which is contained in the canon of Buddhist texts, consisting of the three "baskets" of scriptures (sutras), commentaries (śāstras) and monastic rules (vinaya). When we realize the fact of suffering that is part of every existence, we take our refuge in the Buddha's teaching that helps us to resolve our problems to the point where no more barriers or hindrances remain. The teaching clarifies and resolves all of the thoughts and inclinations in our heart and mind, all the confusion and all of the troubles. If we are able to practice what it tells us to do, it will change our life.

The sangha refers to those who have received and transmitted the teaching of the Buddha until now, the community of the disciples of the Buddha. The lifespan of the Buddha's teaching is supposed to be more than ten thousand years long, and it has already lasted for three thousand years. This means that there are seven thousand more years left of the life of the teaching. Since it is rather difficult for lay people to pass on the teaching in its entirety, we rely on the monastic community to ensure that the teaching will not get lost for future generations. The sangha is comprised of all those who help us understand the teachings and change our lives, the spiritual teachers and wise friends.

In addition to taking our refuge in the Buddha, dharma and sangha, we also take our refuge in our own Buddha-nature. The Buddha taught us that we are all enlightened from the beginning, that we are already Buddha within ourselves. But the question is, what do we need to do to realize this Buddha within ourselves? In addition to the Buddha, we also possess the dharma in our own heart and mind. In other words, our essential nature is the canon containing of all of the scriptures. What do we need to do to understand this canon of scriptures? And finally, our essential nature is also the sangha, our spiritual teacher, which leads us to purity and clarity. Once we realize the teaching of the Buddha, once we fully awaken, we give birth to the Buddha, to the dharma and to the sangha of our own essential nature.

Finally, we also take our refuge in the dharma-body of the Buddha (dharmakāya), the enjoyment-body of the Buddha (samboghakāya) and the transformation-body of the Buddha (nirmanakāya). These are called the three bodies of the Buddha. The dharma-body is the spiritual nature of the entire universe, and every one of us is contained in this dharma-body. When we awaken, all of our confused thoughts simply return back into the enlightened nature of the Buddha. So what are we right now? Right now we are this minute something inside the dharma-body. This is what we are as long as our thoughts have not yet fully awakened to the dharma-body. This is why we want to quickly go back to the Buddha and quickly become enlightened. When all of your fleeting thoughts have arrived home inside the Buddha, you realize the entire vast dharma-body.

The enjoyment-body of the Buddha is the wisdom that arises from the power of contemplation and concentration, that power which realizes the dharma-body. And the transformation-body is the heart of great compassion that we give birth to in enlightenment. The whole universe is nothing but the three bodies of the Buddha, and we ourselves are nothing but the three bodies of the Buddha. As long as we are not yet enlightened, we are called "sentient beings," but once we are enlightened we are called "buddhas." That which clearly grasps the eternal life is called the dharma-body. That which knows that wisdom has no limits or hindrances, that which is able to clear out all troubles and give rise to unlimited wisdom is called the unimpeded enjoyment-body. That which gives birth to the heart of great and all-encompassing compassion is the transformation-body, which is full of blessings.

When we put our trust in the Three Treasures, when we take our refuge in them and rely on them, we will walk on the right path, we will think the right things, and do the right things that are full of blessings. In this way, our lives will become happier and more beautiful, the Pure Land of Buddha Amitābha. Where is this Pure Land to be found? When we study and practice Buddhism with the right view, the right thoughts and the right actions, the Pure Land is here, free of pain. Our pain arises from our wrong way of thinking.

II. Not holding on to views—the Heart Sutra

What is the wrong way of thinking? It is holding onto our views. Our views are intimately connected to the five constituents that make up our existence—namely bodily form, sensation, thought, impulse and consciousness. All five give rise to our views and notions, and all of our views and notions constitute the idea of "I, me, mine." No matter whether we have good thoughts or bad thoughts, constantly giving rise to thoughts is rather tiresome. It is best to let go of those thoughts before they develop into views and notions that we hold on to.

Holding on to views is frayed with troubles, and consciousness in itself is nothing but existence in samsāra, the cycle of birth and death. To what could we compare consciousness to clarify this a bit more? We could compare it to the Internet. When we go on the Internet, we enter into a structure that lets us contact each other and establish an interaction. The function of consciousness is just like this—it creates our relationships and functions as an entry port into life after life. But consciousness itself is nothing but the cycle of birth and death, coming into existence and ceasing to exist.

If therefore we want to be free of this cycle of birth and death, we must transform our consciousness until we reach the state called "No realm of consciousness." This process is taught in the Heart Sutra, which tells us that Bodhisattva Guanzizai (Avalokiteśvara in Sanskrit) "practicing deep prajñāpāramitā, perceived the emptiness of all five constituents and overcame all suffering."

The Bodhisattva Guanzizai (Kanzeon in Japanese) is Bodhisattva Guanshiyin, also called Guanyin for short. The name Guanzizai means "The one whose gaze (guan) is completely free (zizai). Why is the gaze of the bodhisattva free and unimpeded? It is free because of the constant practice of deep prajñāpāramitā, which means "the perfection of wisdom." We achieve the perfection of wisdom by stopping all misleading thoughts and notions and clearly seeing emptiness. If we want overcome all suffering like Bodhisattva Guanyin, we have to see that the five constituents are completely empty of a self. We have to see that ultimately our bodily form, sensations, thoughts, impulses and consciousness are an illusion, a constant process of change, nothing real or lasting.

Now what do we need to do to practice the right and unimpeded view, which is to "perceive the emptiness of all five constituents"? Does it just mean to read the Buddhist scriptures, the Heart Sutra specifically, and to reflect on the meaning of the text? Does this kind of contemplation of the text alone liberate us from misleading thoughts and views, and does it help us to overcome suffering?

Obviously, this alone is not sufficient for our purpose. Stopping all misleading thoughts is an on-going practice, something that we have to engage in all the time. This means that in daily life, whenever feelings and thoughts come up, when the impulse to act on them arises, whenever we do anything, whether it is at work, at home, or somewhere else, we need to be mindful and see whatever happens just like a dream, a bubble, or a flash of lightning, not something to hold on to. If we practice looking at things in this way, if we keep doing it over and over again, our heart will slowly release all of its attachments and be freed of all hindrances. Freed of all hindrances, it will no longer grasp for anything, dwell on anything, or get attached to anything. This is how we are freed of pain—of the pain that we hold in our heart, a pain that results from our mistaken ways of seeing, thinking and acting.

"Bodhisattva Guanzizai perceived the emptiness of all five constituents." Let us ask again what is meant by "emptiness" here? Emptiness means our true essential nature. The text says that our true essential nature "is neither born nor destroyed; neither stained nor pure, neither growing nor lessening." This describes the way of being of our essential nature, its formless form.

In our essential nature, there is "no form, no sensation, no thought, impulse nor consciousness." This means that since there is not a thing, there is no differentiation or distinction either. And thus, there is "no eye, ear, nose, tongue, body, mind," which means there is no activity of the six senses. Without the activity of the six senses there is "no color, sound, smell, taste touch, thing, no realm of sight and no realm of consciousness." This means that the world of phenomena ceases to exist.

Our essential nature needs to learn from the Buddha, so that it may understand, contemplate and practice according to the teaching of the Heart Sutra. How far does our essential nature need to proceed in its practice? It needs to proceed until it reaches that which is called "no realm of sight and no realm of consciousness."

What is meant by "no realm of sight"? It means that we stop perceiving things. And "no realm of consciousness" means that we stop perceiving things: there is nothing at all, no contact point whatsoever remaining for our consciousness. Now our heart no longer produces or fabricates anything at all. With nothing there in our heart, we stop producing karmic actions based on delusion and confusion.

Thus, in the world of no consciousness, nothing exists at all, not even a single thing. You see, our essential nature needs to completely cut off ordinary consciousness to realize this. Thus the text goes on to say that there is "no ignorance and no ending to ignorance, no old age and death and no ending of old age and death, no suffering and no ending to suffering." It is only when there is nothing at all in our heart and mind that we will we be freed from birth, old age, illness and death. There will be no more ignorance, since ignorance means trouble—birth and death. In other words, without ignorance, there will not be any birth, old age, illness and death. Without ignorance, there is also no ending to ignorance—there is nothing we need to do to end ignorance; since it is already cut off. Without birth, old age and death, there is no ending of these things either, since it they have already ended. The same goes for suffering. When there is no more suffering caused by ignorance, there is also no ending to suffering, since it has already ended.

The text continues to say, "There is no path, no wisdom and no gain." This means that there is no suffering, no origin of suffering, no ending of suffering—in other words, there is neither the cycle of rebirth nor the practice of ending it. "No wisdom and no gain" means that there is nothing at all which we could attain. There is nothing to gain in emptiness, and there is nothing to obstruct it either.

"Since there is nothing to gain," the text continues, "the bodhisattva lives this prajñāpāramitā with no hindrance of mind, no hindrance, therefore no fear. Far from all such delusions, nirvāna is already here. All past, present and future buddhas practice this and attain the supreme, perfect way." Prajñāpāramitā, the highest wisdom, is the ability to look at the many objects and happenings of the phenomenal world in a way that sees through them until there is nothing at all left and everything is devoid of solidity, not really existing. It means to "see all conditioned things as AN ILLUSION, A DEWDROP, A BUBBLE / A DREAM, A CLOUD, A FLASH OF LIGHTNING." Again, this way of looking, of contemplating things in our heart and mind, is what we have to constantly practice in our daily life, no matter what the circumstances. And this practice is the "supreme, perfect way" which is Right Thought. Prajñāpāramitā, completely seeing through everything, is the right view which gives rise to Right Thought.

Not holding on to views then means that we have to start from the first link in the Eightfold Noble Path taught by the Buddha, namely from Right View, and see with the Buddha's own eyes ourselves. How do we develop the Right View right from the beginning? First of all we need to know that every time a wrong thought rears its head we are headed for trouble. Every time we do the wrong things, we are headed for trouble. But if every time we give rise to the right thought, based on the right view, we are headed for happiness.

Developing the Right View as expounded in the Heart Sutra, developing a gaze that is free and unimpeded, is nothing but the dharma—the teaching. Only when we fully comprehend and practice the dharma are we able to return to that in each of us that is unborn and never dies, that which is not arising and not subsiding, because life and death, arising and subsiding are nothing but our own wrong notions.

When the Buddha awakened under the Bodhi tree, he saw that all beings already have the power and wisdom of the Thus Come One (Tathāgatha), but that they are not as fully liberated and free as the Awakened One because of the wrong notions and ideas that they keep holding on to. This means that all of us, without exception, are endowed with Buddha-nature from the start, and that all we need to do is to see it, understand it and get to know it. When you proceed step by step according to the teaching of the Buddha, you will get to know yourself more and more clearly. What do I mean by "yourself"? By this I mean your Buddha-nature. Everybody has Buddha-nature, but why don't you realize it is right here? Is it because you do not know what it means? But if you know what it means and go to explore it more and more deeply, if you endeavor to realize it, you will awaken without fail and become a Buddha yourself.

III. Precepts (*sīla*), Concentration (*dhyāna*) and Wisdom (*prajñā*)

Once we have taken our refuge in the Three Treasures, we are encouraged to take up the practice of keeping the precepts. This is how I proceeded as well after becoming ordained as a monk. When I first embarked on my ascetic practice in the dilapidated old house in the outskirts of Taipei, I was constantly thinking about the meaning of human life. How could I overcome all of the troubles and pains that are like dreams and bubbles? I knew that the only way to do this was to be vigorous in my practice; I needed to subdue my body and rein in my mind to rediscover the luminous wisdom of the heart, which dissolves all pain. The first step on this path, the first discipline, is keeping the precepts.

What is the meaning of the precepts? The precepts mean that I know life will necessarily entail many tensions and conflicts and that my character, my habits and my ways of thinking are prone to producing unwholesome karmic seeds. Keeping the precepts then simply means that we reduce the opportunities for ourselves to produce unwholesome karmic actions, and we don't give others the opportunity to produce unwholesome karmic actions either. In other words, we refrain from "doing all that is unwholesome," and commit to "doing all that is wholesome." Thus we cease producing troubles and attain joy. All that is good and wholesome makes us into happy people, and by contrast, all that is bad and unwholesome makes us into people with worries and troubles.

The precepts are principles upon which we base our lives, and they are the rules that show us how to live it well. If we keep the rules, we cease creating so many troubles and conflicts with others. Let us then use our lives to study the principles and keep the rules, and not merely to produce one trouble after another.

What do the precepts entail? The Buddha told us that if we want to develop a very good character, we have to observe the following five basic five precepts: 1) do not kill, 2) do not steal, 3) do not engage in improper sexual conduct, 4) do not make false statements, and 5) do not take intoxicants. There are also the Bodhisattva precepts and the precepts for the nuns and monks.

If we can keep these basic five precepts, we will never fall into the three bad realms of rebirth—namely into hell, into the realm of the hungry ghosts or into the realm of the animals. We will instead reap the benefits of being born into the three good realms—those of the human beings, the titans and the gods.

The second discipline is concentration (dhyāna). Our heart and mind are of a habitual nature, just like fire that likes to burn things, or just like water that likes to move and flow, or like wind that likes to blow. Everything has its own habitual nature, so how can we change our own habitual tendencies? We need to clean out those habitual tendencies if we want to be able to clearly see our original nature. You will not find your face reflected in mud, but only in water that is pure and pristine. When we keep the precepts, the water of our habitual nature will become pure, so that we will slowly come to behold our own Buddha nature.

We need to practice concentration because our heart and mind are so fickle, unruly and all over the place. With concentration in meditation, our heart and mind will slowly calm down. As long as we still produce so many random and misleading thoughts, we will not be able to see our original nature. Therefore we need to practice keeping the precepts, and practice concentration.

Concentration means to pacify our heart and mind, to guide and tame them and to be in charge of them—not the other way round. Are you able to do this—to be in charge of your heart and mind? That is why we need the precepts to rein them in, and then the stability in concentration to harmonize them. The precepts help control the heart and mind, and concentration helps to attune them gradually, step by step, attuning them again and again until they listen to you. When your heart and mind completely listen to you, you will be the happiest person in the world—nobody could be happier than you. Your heart and mind need to become even softer than a purring cat. Are not some among you afraid of petting a cat, since it might scratch you? Most of the time the cat is gentle and soft, and once you have tuned your own heart into that kind of softness, it will be joyful and at ease.

But even if we have practiced keeping the precepts and concentration, even if our heart and mind have softened a bit, we may still not be able to completely cut out our delusions and troubles. This is why we need wisdom. Wisdom refers to what we think. There are a myriad of things in this universe, but there is no way for us to mentally penetrate and understand all of them. How could we understand so many things? Wisdom means that we want to see through all of these things, penetrate them in our thinking, and then let go of them. But why can we not let go of them right now? Simply because we do not possess that wisdom: namely the wisdom of seeing through them, mentally penetrating and letting go of them. And so we carry these things with us like a stone around our necks, or like a big heap of thorns that prick us whenever we move. We cry out, "It hurts, it hurts!" But still we cannot let go, since we don't really want to let go. And so we keep crying, "Ouch, ouch—it's so painful!"

Wisdom helps us to pull out the thorns that prick us and to discard them; it helps us to no longer feel so much pain, to no longer hold on to things. But now, you are still collecting and holding on to those things, those things that are so painful, those things that give you so many troubles. You need wisdom to let go of those attachments and entanglements.

What do we need to do to develop wisdom? We simply need to consult the Buddhist scriptures, listen to the words of wise and holy ones and practice what they tell us to do. In other words, we need to acquire wisdom through listening to dharma talks and through the study of the scriptures. When we listen to a teacher expounding the dharma, it can help us to dissolve our doubts and confusion. This is the reason why we listen to a teacher. When our doubts and delusions have been dissolved, we are as free as a fish that has been thrown back into the water. As long as our delusions have not yet been dispelled, we get entangled in them, bound and confused by anything that rises before our eyes, and we make ourselves suffer. Therefore we should take our refuge in the Three Treasures and practice the precepts, concentration and wisdom.

If we practice in this way, we will be able to become saints! What do I mean by this? A person who has attained the fruit of sainthood has tapped into the core energy of the whole universe. You need to enter into and become this core energy; you need to become the very center of the universe. As long as we have not yet accessed this core energy, we are just like dust and ashes being blown around by the wind, leading very unsteady and unstable lives that lack a firm center. When we become fully accomplished saints—arhats—we will reach nirvāna. Nirvāna is the central energy of the universe, its central force, the place that each and every one of us will necessarily return to. As long as we have not yet been able to return home, we will feel lonely and disconnected, and this is the reason why we have to always come back to the basic and central thought, which is nirvāna. Once we have reached nirvāna we will be able to overcome birth and death, but only then. However, if our wisdom is not yet sufficient, complete liberation will be out of our reach.

To develop that kind of perfect wisdom (prajñāpāramitā), we have to practice the way of the bodhisattva. Just reading the scriptures is not enough. Only practicing the way of the bodhisattva will help us understand and develop perfect wisdom; and it is only through perfect wisdom that we can dissolve all of our doubts and delusions. Right now our views are deluded and our thoughts are deluded as well. Think about it—are all of these delusions not numberless—just like grains of sand and dust? In the bodhisattva vows we say: "Delusions are numberless. I vow to end them." When will we start with our study and practice? If we don't start right now, will we have enough time left for it later?

So when we want to study Buddhism, we want to achieve nirvāna and reach enlightenment; we want to practice the way of the bodhisattva. What is the meaning of nirvāna? It means to be become free from birth and death. And practicing the way of the bodhisattva means becoming a Buddha. And what is the meaning of becoming a Buddha? It means benefitting others, and by doing so, benefitting oneself. When we benefit others we develop perfect wisdom, and when we benefit ourselves through benefitting others, we achieve nirvāna. So when we practice benefitting ourselves we will ultimately reach nirvāna, and when we practice benefitting others, we will ultimately become like the Buddha. Like the Buddha, we will answer all questions from the place of knowing, and like the Buddha, we will say all things from the place of knowing. No matter from which direction things come at us, there will never be a problem or moment of hesitation, since there is not a thing in the world that would stupefy the Buddha. Buddha means omniscient wisdom.

IV. The three bodies of the Buddha

The Buddha has made this world into the ground for enlightenment. Not only this world but the whole universe is the ground for enlightenment, the land of the Buddha.

What do I mean by "the land of the Buddha?" It means the three bodies of the Buddha in which we take our refuge—namely the dharma-body, the enjoyment-body and the transformation-body as I already explained earlier. All of us, every one without exception, are endowed with these three bodies. We have this life that is eternal and will never die, but we usually are not aware of it. That is the dharma-body—the one that we are not aware of. The enjoyment-body is endowed with a mind of wisdom, and what we call the transformation-body is all of the constant interactions and changes in our lives.

What we need to realize is the dharma-body of the Buddha, the body that each of us possesses, the one that never dies, the eternal spirit, the eternal nature of enlightenment, the eternal Buddha-nature. All you need to do to realize it is to be willing to study Buddhism and learn from the Buddha; to be willing to turn your head around and look at your own dharma-body, namely at the Buddha in yourself.

The second body, namely the enjoyment-body is the mind of wisdom. Again, what do I mean by wisdom? Wisdom means that we no longer have any hindrances or blockages in our heart and mind. We are free of troubles, and everything is clear and perfectly understood.

The third body is a heart of compassion, which takes all living beings as one's own transformation-body, as the very ground that transforms everything through compassion. All living beings are the very ground which the Buddha provides for us to be transformed and develop a heart of great compassion. Sometimes we look at living beings and others as if they existed outside of us. But this is not the case at all—they are not separate from us; they are inside us. If we realize this and are able to transform our own heart and mind into great compassion, it is the transformation-body. Furthermore, if we can transform our troubles into wisdom, it is the enjoyment-body, and if we can transform these two bodies that still possess form into the body that no longer has any form, it is the dharma-body, the one that never dies, the one that all of us possess. But at this point, we are simply still confused about this— that is all.

All of us are dwelling in the land of the Buddha. So what are we supposed to do here? Those of us who study Buddhism are supposed to learn to do three things here: the work of the dharma-body, the work of the enjoyment-body and the work of the transformation-body. This means that we no longer live by the power of karma, but by the power of the vow to achieve enlightenment. The vow to achieve enlightenment means the vow to free all sentient beings, to end all delusions and to study the teachings of the Buddha. Dwelling in the land of the Buddha, we endeavor every day to transform the power of karma into the power of the vow, so that we live a life that is no longer constricted by time but is an eternal life that fully embodies our omniscient, enlightened nature.

Dwelling in the land of the Buddha, what does our work consist of?

Being clearly aware of the law of cause and effect, this work consists of engaging in actions that are full of blessings and wisdom. Actions that are full of blessings allow us to generously give of ourselves and constantly learn how to generate happiness for others. This is compassion. Actions that are full of wisdom allow us to be able to often let go of our troubles and worries, being able to lighten up. This is what we practice in meditation and through altruism. Blessings are compassion; wisdom is letting go. Let us therefore often carry out actions that are full of compassion and giving, which will create blessings and wisdom. Wisdom means untying the fetters of our troubles, and blessings mean a life that goes smoothly, a life in which nothing is lacking. Often engaging in actions that are compassionate and altruistic is called the path of the bodhisattva. The bodhisattva helps all sentient beings to be free of suffering and achieve happiness.

When Buddha Śākyamuni practiced the way of the bodhisattva, he felt that every breath he took in this life was not just for himself, but for all sentient beings. When we can do likewise in our own practice, we will feel that our burden lightens and our heart becomes settled and at peace. If you can breathe in and breathe out for the sake of others, if you can take every breath in order to benefit them, you will fully develop the heart of enlightenment. By fully embracing others you overcome yourself.

All of us have in us the seeds to become a fully realized Buddha, and we need to water and nourish those seeds so that they may fully develop and blossom. As a fully realized Buddha we possess perfect wisdom (prajñāpāramitā), a full understanding of the truth about the universe and about human life. Understanding the truth about the universe means that we know what this universe consists of, how it came into existence and how it brought forth this world that we live in. At that moment in which we reach full realization, our knowledge about this life is complete. Now we clearly know where this life is coming from, where it is going and why we are here. Now we know our "original face before our parents were born," and are freed of pain, just like Bodhisattva Avalokiteśvara. The most direct way to reach this realization is through the practice of Chan.

Chapter 4

TAKING THE PATH OF CHAN

What is it that we look for when we start engaging ourselves in the practice of Chan meditation? Are we not searching for that which is most real in life so that we can live out our lives from there?

We need to realize that this body of ours is not real—it is a moving and changing entity that is fashioned by karmic memory. If our memory is already unreliable and unreal then how much more so is our body? What then is most real in life? It is our original face - in the language of Chan "our face before our parents were born." Our original face is neither our memory nor our body; it is not this body of memory that we so like to cling to, this body of life. Memory is life in action, a life that is composed of causes and conditions. Our body is composed of causes and conditions; our thoughts are composed of causes and conditions; our entire life is composed of causes and conditions.

Now all of these karmic compositions are illusory, and yet we live in the midst of this illusion, unable to extricate ourselves from it. And so we live together with this illusion, die together with this illusion, and come back again together with this illusion. Our feelings are tied to this illusion: the feeling of life, the feeling of perishing, the feeling of death and the feeling of rebirth. Confused by and suffering from these illusions we create more karma, both good and bad, and become entangled with the lives of others, producing such emotions as love and hate, emotions that we hold on to for dear life. These kinds of emotions create a dynamic energy among us, namely that energy which is called samsāra.

So how do we let go of our attachment to feelings, which keeps us in the cycle of rebirth in samsāra? How do we redirect our gaze from the material world outside with its fleeting things, and from our emotions that are tied to these things, to the inside where we will find the source of freedom? It is by searching for our original face. Chan is the search for our original face. The purpose of Chan is to enlighten our heart and mind and to see our true nature. Enlightening our heart and mind and seeing our true nature is seeing our original face. Our original face is beyond this changing body of ours, this body of memory; it is beyond this web-like memory, beyond the entanglements with this structure of life. Our original face is our nature of enlightenment, that which has been there from the beginning. What is the meaning of enlightenment? It is that in us which is able to investigate, to understand, to experience and to know clearly.

It is not easy for us to be born as a human being; it is not easy to receive this body of ours. It is an occurrence as rare as a single sand in comparison with the millions and millions of others that line a seashore. The Buddha once picked up a handful of dirt and told his disciples that those who attain human rebirth are as few as a handful of dirt in comparison to the entire earth. It is only the human among the six realms of sentient beings that is capable of realizing enlightenment. Since we are now fortunate enough to have this very rare human body, with a heart and mind that are able to investigate, understand, experience and know, we should not waste this precious opportunity to free ourselves from birth and death and overcome our troubles.

When I say "to free ourselves from birth and death," what do I mean by it? What is it that is born and dies? Our memory is born and dies, and our body is born and dies. But neither one of them, neither our memory nor our body are our original face. If therefore we want to find our original face, we should start with the practice of Chan. We should start forming the habit of constantly dwelling in the awakened clarity of Chan practice rather than the habit of being caught up in our body and memories. When you are caught up in your body and memories, it means life in samsāra. But when you practice Chan, you return to your original face. When you concentrate on breathing in and breathing out and on deeply listening to silence, ask yourself if it is your body or your memory that is doing this practice. If it is neither one of them, then resolve to cultivate the habit of resting in awakening and clear understanding, not the habit of getting caught up in illusions and attachments.

Life in samsāra is nothing but an engrained habit—if it is our habit to turn with the wheel of coming and going, we will be coming and going. If we make troubles into our habit, if we get caught up in our entanglements—in distinguishing between good and bad, yes and no, what we like and what he hate—then we will be stuck there, making the rounds of birth and death. But if we make our original face, that which is unborn and never dies, into our habit, we are freed from birth and death.

I.   Stopping (shamatā) and Seeing (vipassanā)

So how can we get rid of our attachment to illusions, how can we cut them off once and for all as if with a knife? The cutting knife is the practice of Chan—which pierces through all of our delusions if we engage ourselves in it diligently. To practice Chan is not like eating snacks— it is the fruit of a life of tilling the ground of our true nature. We need time, patience and the right environment to engage in this practice. And we need a mind that is focused.

Our fleeting thoughts are like the distracting noises that we can hear outside when we sit quietly in meditation—voices, music, the sound of cars passing by. Is our attention not constantly drifting towards those noises, rather than staying with the practice? The power of karma is like these distracting noises from outside that keep getting our attention, making it difficult for us to return to our practice and to come home to our origin. So what do we need to do to let our heart and mind return to our original face?

We have to gradually eliminate all that which is causing disturbances to our practice, step by step purifying ourselves in the process until we reach the clarity of enlightenment and live our lives in its light. This means that we are no longer trapped in the artificial mental structures that we have spun for ourselves like a spider web through our thoughts and concepts. It means that we have returned to the purity and simplicity of our original face.

Chan offers us different ways of practice to help us enlighten our heart and see our true nature, to return home to our original face, but they essentially all come back to two basic methods, namely stopping (shamatā) and seeing (vipassanā). Stopping means to rein in the constant flow of our thoughts through concentration and bring our heart and mind to a place of inner stillness. In other words, it means concentrating our heart and mind on one point to let them become settled. Our heart and mind are always naturally distracted and do not easily cooperate in concentration. But without concentration it is impossible for us to focus, to think clearly, to contemplate deeply and to develop full understanding. When we are unable to think clearly, to contemplate deeply and to develop full understanding, we cannot reach enlightenment.

When we practice stopping, our mind quits producing distractive thoughts and calms down just like the waves of the ocean quiet down when the wind stops blowing. Once your mind reaches the place of inner stillness, it becomes clear and radiant like a mirror that clearly reflects everything that exists without making any distinctions.

Seeing means to throw off body and mind. When we throw off body and mind, we are aware that there is nothing for us to attain. We look at everything that exists in the universe in the light of wisdom and clearly recognize that all of it is marked by change and impermanence and that all that happens is interdependent. We see that everything is instantaneous, short-lived and already over before we can grasp it; therefore there is not a single thing for us to attain, to gain or to hold on to. We see everything as a mirage, an illusion. This also pertains to our concept of time. Time is nothing more than coming into existence and ceasing to exist, instant by instant, between birth and death. If we are able to stop and see time, knowing what it is, then we are no longer confined by it. And when we clearly see the interdependent and conditioned nature of all that arises, we attain the mirror-like wisdom of the heart that equally illuminates everything.

Seeing is precisely what the Heart Sutra is teaching us about, as it explains how we proceed from perceiving the emptiness of our body, sensations, thoughts, impulses and consciousness until we arrive at the realm of no sight and no consciousness, at the realm of nothing there at all, where there is no "touch-point" for our consciousness remaining.

When we are successful in practicing stopping, we no longer give birth to so many misleading and distracting thoughts. And when we are successful in practicing seeing, our gaze is free and unimpeded like that of Bodhisattva Guanyin. Stopping and seeing function together like two wheels on a cart—stopping our discursive mind in meditation helps us to develop mirror-like wisdom, and mirror-like wisdom helps us to stop the workings of the discursive mind. There is no longer any difference between them: concentration is wisdom—and wisdom is concentration. When we reach this state of concentration we naturally and freely bring forth the light of our original face and radiate the peace and stillness of the spirit.

II.   Finding your original face—a transmission outside of the scriptures

There are two major types or ways of meditation that we practice in the Chan tradition. One is called the "Chan of the patriarchs," which involves working with a gongan (called kōan in Japanese). A gongan is a paradoxical phrase from a teaching by a Chan patriarch or teacher which cuts through the workings of the conceptual mind and helps to trigger insight in the student. "What is your original face before your parents were born?" is such a phrase which helps you return to your original true self, the one that has always been there, even before you were born. Your original self has many names, including God, Buddha or Allah. This original Self of yours that you are seeking is nothing other than the nature of reality, the nature of the universe itself.

The other type of meditation centers on the practice of "silent illumination," in which we quietly and diligently observe our enlightened nature during meditation. Both methods go well together—working with a gongan and quietly observing our enlightened nature complement each other. In Chan, the work with a gongan is mainly used in the Linji (Rinzai in Japanese) School, while the quiet illumination is the method employed by the Caodong (Sōtō School). The Rinzai school likes to emphasizes "sudden enlightenment", while the emphasis of the Caodong school is on "gradual enlightenment."

The purpose of each type of Chan meditation is to enlighten our heart and mind, to realize our true nature and to lead an awakened life. When we sit in Chan meditation, we sit in the light of our enlightened nature, which can never be extinguished, and tend to its flame. That light was passed on in a mind-to-mind, heart-to-heart transmission from Buddha to Mahakāśyapā, his senior disciple who became the second Patriarch in the Chan lineage.

Buddha Śākyamuni had two senior disciples called Ânanda and Mahakāśyapā. Ânanda always kept close to the Buddha and memorized every word that the Buddha ever spoke. This is why the scriptures, which are the words memorized by Ânanda, handed down to us in written form, always start with "Thus I have heard." Differently from Ânanda, Mahakāśyapā liked to go off to the forest all by himself and practice strict ascetic meditation in seclusion. He was very serious and never smiled.

One day, the Buddha dwelt on Vulture Peak, the mountain in northern India where he preached the Lotus Sutra, ready to give a dharma talk to the great assembly of his disciples, which included the most highly accomplished and enlightened practitioners. The audience was waiting for him to start his teaching. Without saying anything, the Buddha just lifted up a white flower, twirled it around and smiled. Everyone in the big audience was silent, wondering what the Buddha was doing, and only Mahakāśyapā broke into a broad smile. What was he smiling about? And what did Mahakāśyapā realize? Into the silence, the Buddha spoke and said, "I have the treasury of the true dharma eye, the marvelous mind of nirvāna, the true formless form, and the subtle dharma gate, which is independent of words and concepts and transmitted outside of the scriptures. This I have just entrusted to Mahakāśyapā."

When Mahakāśyapā looked at the flower, he realized the wonderful mind of nirvāna, which the Buddha intimately passed on to him, and saw that the true form is no form, that form is emptiness. It was a moment of mind touching mind, of mind recognizing mind, of mind imprinting on mind. The mind of nirvāna can never fully be captured in words or concepts; it can only be experienced in that moment of awakening which fully reveals your original face. This fact is expressed in the four principles of Chan: It is a transmission outside of the scriptures; it does not rely on words and concepts; it is passed on in a mind-to-mind transmission; it helps you to awaken to your true Self and become a Buddha yourself.

Our original face is nothing other than the "treasury of the true dharma eye," which means seeing things as they really are. It is "the marvelous mind of nirvāna", which is unborn, which never ceases and which has immeasurable virtues and functions. It is "the true formless form, and the subtle dharma gate which is independent of words and concepts and transmitted outside of the scriptures." These principles of Chan are nothing but our original face.

III. Cultivating Samādhi through listening to Silence

When I practiced Chan by myself in the graveyard for ten years and later on in the mountain cave for an additional two years, I did not have a teacher nearby who was guiding me, but I followed the example and teaching of great ascetic masters like Mahakāśyapā who had taken up this kind of severe practice before me. Most of all, I took my spiritual recourse to the Bodhisattva Guanyin and started devoting myself to the method that Guanyin teaches in the Śūrangama Sutra. This method, which is called "Perfect Penetration through Hearing," does not rely on any words or concepts, but on listening to silence. Listening to silence is a method that helps us enter deeply into samādhi and to fully realize our enlightened nature. Since it is the very method that brought me to spiritual realization, I teach this method to all of my students.

The Śūrangama Sutra describes how Bodhisattva Guanyin, who was dwelling on an island, listened to the sound of the waves washing up against the rocks on the shore. As Guanyin was fully absorbed in listening to the waves as they rose and splashed against the rocks then receded into silence over and over again—rising and receding, rising and receding—every sound eventually became silent as it reached Guanyin's ears. In the sutra, this process of listening until no more sound is heard is called "Entering the stream of the self-nature of hearing." Guanyin describes this process in the sutra as follows:

"I entered into the stream of the self-nature of hearing, and thereby eliminated the sound of what was heard. When I proceeded from this inner stillness both sounds and silence ceased to arise. Advancing in this way, both hearing and what was heard melted away and disappeared. When hearing and what is heard are both forgotten, the sense of hearing leaves no impression in the mind."

This describes a process of listening to silence in which you simply listen without attaching to sound, without attaching to silence, without attaching to a difference between sound and silence, without attaching to anything at all. If you are able to listen in this way, you eventually reach a point where listening occurs but no longer has an object. In other words, there is still awareness, but that what you are aware of is empty. The object of awareness has dropped away, but awareness remains.

As the text says, "When both awareness and the objects of awareness become empty, then emptiness and awareness merge and reach a state of absolute perfection." It is at this point, when emptiness and your awareness of it completely match, that your awareness is transformed into emptiness. But even then you cannot hold on to that experience of emptiness; you need to let go of it completely too—by listening even more. This is what the text is telling us, saying, "When emptiness and what is being emptied are both extinguished, then birth and death, arising and extinction are naturally extinguished." In other words, when there is no awareness of either emptiness or form, when there is no mental distinction between them remaining whatsoever, and you have experienced complete stillness at the core of everything, then you have returned to your original face. It is at this point of return that you fully comprehend samsāra and are liberated from it.

The process of listening described by Bodhisattva Guanyin in the Śūraṅgama Sutra is a process of deeply entering into samādhi. Entering into samādhi means entering into liberation. Samādhi is a state in which our heart and mind are no longer aroused, in which they are no longer moving at all. The process to arrive at this stage is not so easy—it takes quite some time. How long do you think it would take you to listen to the sound of the waves like Bodhisattva Guanyin until your mind no longer moves?

Cultivating samādhi is the one and only thing that I practiced all day and all night long during the time that I spent in the graveyard and then in the cave. What else would I have done there? There are different words used for samādhi in the scriptures: it is called the "right way of taking something in" or the "right way of concentration." The word "right" is used here in the sense of being fully at rest in our enlightened nature and letting every thought return to it. The "right way of taking something in" means not to take anything in at all, and the "right way of concentration" means to leave all things of the phenomenal world completely behind. Samādhi is the state in which your heart and mind stop producing any kind of intentional action, the state in which they are fully immersed in non-action (wu-wei).

One example of this state of samādhi is writing calligraphy in a way that flows so naturally and beautifully that your heart and mind are the calligraphy, and the calligraphy is your heart and mind. This means that there is no longer any difference between them. In this state, there is no longer any difference between being and non-being. Being is that which is visible, that which we see with our eyes; non-being is the thought that we hold in our heart, namely the thought of nothingness, of emptiness. When you look at anything, it is important to neither take it from the side of being, nor from the side of nothingness, but to rest in your enlightened nature. Resting in your enlightened nature means not to run anywhere else—neither to the side of being nor to the side on non-being.

If you do not rest in your enlightened nature, you either get involved with things, or hold on to nothingness. Of course it is important for us to understand emptiness, because this is the only way to overcome our grasping heart and mind. When we clearly understand that all the illusions of the phenomenal world will melt away one by one like a piece of ice, we finally see emptiness. In other words, we move from seeing something to seeing nothing. It is easy to think that once our heart and mind are no longer attached to anything we should dwell in emptiness, since everything is empty anyway. If you think this way, it is wrong. Do not dwell in being, and do not dwell in emptiness, but dwell in non-dwelling. Non-dwelling is another word for samādhi.

There are some people who are able to reach entry into samādhi through repeating the name of Buddha Amitābha. If you repeat the name of the Buddha, realizing there is no past, there is no future and there is also no present—if your one period of sitting in meditation becomes three or even seven days long, without any thought of food, nor any notion of hot or cold—then you have so deeply entered into samādhi that you might be able to develop the power of mental penetration that is written about in the scriptures. We all have the capacity of mental penetration, but we usually don't practice enough to experience it. With the power of mental penetration your sense of hearing will have no more obstacles remaining. With the removal of all obstacles you will be able to hear everything in the whole universe with all of its galaxies, which is so much bigger than just this small world of ours. Not only will you be able to hear everything that is beyond this world, but also everything in this world; you will be able to hear and understand the conversation of the ants on the ground, or of the birds in the air. This is possible because, with the power of samādhi, the waves of your heart and mind become so finely attuned and subtle that they intimately connect with the heart waves emitted by others. Your own heart and mind become the receptor for all of these different waves, and you do not need words or language to understand them. But now we are still far from developing that kind of mental penetration, because the waves of our own heart and mind are not yet subtle enough.

Chan is the method to refine our heart and mind, to refine every single thought that arises. As we keep refining thought after thought, they become more and more subtle, more and more attuned to stillness and emptiness. Once your thoughts, your heart and your mind are attuned to stillness and emptiness, they are attuned to nothingness. You have to refine your mind until it proceeds from stillness and emptiness to nothingness. This is how you have to practice the inner attunement.

The method to practice this inner refinement, of dissolving everything that is coarse and rough, is listening to silence. Listening to silence means letting our mind that constantly gives rise to things, to birth and death, quiet down until nothing arises anymore. It is to use a heart of stillness to abolish the mind that gives rise to things. It is to use a heart of non-discrimination, so that we do not make any distinctions between sounds and silence. When we listen with a mind that makes distinctions, our practice is not the correct one. Our organ of hearing is all embracing and complete – it does not discriminate between sounds. When we practice long enough in concentrating on hearing itself, not on the object of hearing, our hearing becomes transformed into samādhi.

With samādhi we realize how we are usually confined by our discriminating mind. For example, we usually think we cannot pass through a wall or a group of people, and indeed we cannot do this, because we are blocked by our discriminating mind. But if you practice listening to silence until you succeed in listening without making any distinctions, which happens in samādhi, you develop the power of liberation. Now you are no longer pushed around by material things, but you are the one who moves and transforms them. Without a discriminating mind, you can look at a wall and pass right through it, since you fully realize it is empty. There are some advanced practitioners who are able to freely roam in the empty sky, since they don't hold on to a notion of emptiness. And they can freely pass through walls, because they don't have the mistaken notion of material existence as being. So how should one listen to silence? Listen to emptiness. And how should one think? Think emptiness. And how should one practice? Practice resting in emptiness.

IV. The four steps of the Listening to Silence Practice

It is while I was practicing the method of listening to silence in the graveyard that I developed a four step method that helps us to regulate our breath and settle our body and mind before we start listening to silence. The first three steps in this method are geared towards stopping (shamatā) our distracted and dispersed mind by concentrating it on one point, and the fourth step is geared toward seeing (vipassanā) emptiness through the stillness of our heart and mind. I will now explain these steps one by one.

1) Taking seven deep breaths

When we begin our meditation, it is important that we sit in a stable position. Our back should be straight, our chin slightly tucked in, and our eyes partly open, without focusing on anything in particular, to forestall daydreaming. Our mouth is closed, with the tongue slightly touching the upper palate. When we sit down we can easily begin to feel drowsy because the cells in our body are tired, whether it is from a cold, or from having eaten too much or from a busy day. Therefore it is important to prepare our meditation well by deeply breathing in and out. When we breathe in, we breathe in fresh energy (chi), and when we breathe out, we expel stale energy. Breathe in from the dantian, the energy center located right under the navel. It is from here that we draw up the air and feel it pass through our throat as we are breathing in. Then we breathe out through our nose. With each inhale, be aware of the air passing through your throat, and be aware how it passes through the nose with each exhale. It is important to breathe slowly and deeply while keeping your chin slightly tucked in, since it is difficult to breathe in this way if you are looking up. This way of breathing is derived from an Indian Yoga practice, and we can take recourse of it every time that we feel drowsy during meditation.

2) Moving the attention from the eyes to the nose, mouth and heart

This method is especially geared towards reining in our monkey mind that we find so difficult to control. We start by gently moving the attention from the eyes to the area under the nose, where we are breathing in and out, and let it rest there for a while. From there we move the attention on to the mouth, and feel our mouths Finally we move our attention from our mouth to our heart and hold no thoughts or images whatsoever in our heart. Then we start all over again from the eyes.

This process is expressed thusly: the eyes see the nose, the nose sees the mouth and the mouth sees the heart. Do the nose or the mouth have eyes? Of course not—the eyes that we are speaking about here are our inner eyes, namely the eyes of our mind and heart. Now the eye of the heart looks at the heart and sees nothing there to see, no thoughts or images. The heart does not get involved with anything; it is free from all grasping, and it does not dwell on anything. In Buddhist terms we say that the heart does not get involved with any karmic seeds or conditions.

Now there is no set speed for each step of the movement. Adjust your own speed, as long as you remain mindful of each step. If you go too fast, you might miss a step, and if you go to slow, you might lose attention. The whole movement is a process of reining in the restless heart and mind, of bringing them back home.

3) Observing the breath

Just breathing in and breathing out seems very simple. Most methods geared to achieve stopping and seeing take their departure point from the breath. Breath is intimately connected to everything—to our own lives and every other life in the universe. So when we speak about "observing the breath," what does it really mean and entail? It means letting our heart and mind rest on the breath; it means "collecting" the mind by breathing in and out; it means letting the breath and mind become one, not two; it means letting the mind exactly be where the breath is, without the slightest gap. When we are too intent on taking hold of our breath, we miss it, and when we are too relaxed, our breath escapes to who knows where. So when contemplating the breath, do not try to force it, but also do not be too relaxed either. Observe the breath with the awareness of your heart, that innate awareness that each of us possesses. Try to fasten that inner awareness on the breath.

The mind keeps running all over the place like a monkey. If we can fasten the mind on the breath, then we fasten the monkey there, so that it keeps moving along with the breath—in and out, in and out—but it no longer runs off very far away. After some time, the monkey gets used to this and feels that staying with the movement of the breath is natural and comfortable. When you reach this state where the monkey no longer feels bound by the breath, but enjoys staying there, then you have reached the stage of stopping, in which your awareness gently rests on the breath. When we sit well and diligently in meditation for a long time, we will experience the breath as a body of light. But now, a "body of light" is still just a notion in our mind, since we have not yet developed the power of samādhi which generates this kind of experience.

When you observe your breath and notice that it is rough, ask yourself why it is rough; if it is smooth, ask why it is smooth; if it is deep, ask why it is deep; if it is shallow, ask why it is shallow; if it is dry, ask why it feels dry; if it is moist, ask why it feels moist; if it is cool, ask why it feels cool; or if it is warm, ask why it feels warm. As you observe your breath in this manner, you build up the power of concentration. If you don't do it, you will find it difficult to keep sitting, since our heart and mind always like to move and run somewhere else. Because of this it is important to keep up a regular practice of minutely observing the breath in meditation.

4) Listening to silence

While the previous three steps are intended to stop (shamatā) the wandering mind by letting it rest on the breath, the fourth step of listening has more to do with seeing (vipassanā). Our ears are in a state of listening 24-hours a day. But this state of listening is a state in which we make mental distinctions. In this state our minds actively distinguish between sounds, and this state of mental activity is always short-lived and changing. Through listening to silence, we leave behind the state of mental distinction and fully return to our original self. So when we listen to silence, we move our mind deeply inside that silence and see with the eyes of the stilled mind. The sense of hearing is our sharpest sense, and this is the reason why Bodhisattva Guanyin used the method of "entering the stream of the self-nature of hearing" to reach enlightenment.

In preparation, we start by relaxing our ears, our heads, our necks, our shoulders, our entire bodies and every cell in our bodies; and we make every cell smile. We quiet down completely and let everything else quiet down. When we hear sounds from the outside, like the sounds of a voice or the noise of a car passing by, we listen to them as the sound of silence. If we listen to distracting noises as silence, they will be silent. However if we listen to them as noise and disturbance, they will be noise and disturbance. Once we attach our mind to noise, we evoke thoughts, feelings and worries again. Rather than being trapped in this, let everything simply quiet down and feel the silence: there is no longer anything here that is not quiet. Keep listening to the sound of silence in everything, staying completely relaxed. The mountains and rivers, the great wide earth, the sky, the whole universe has quieted down; everything is in deep silence. Perceive that deep silence in yourself.

What is the meaning of deep silence? It means that there is no sound whatsoever, and when we listen, we listen to the sound of no sound. As we listen, every thought returns into silence and becomes still. It is important that we do not try to force anything when listening, but that we remain relaxed and listen in a natural way. Otherwise we might develop pain in our ears or even get a headache.

There are also four steps in listening to silence. The first one is to find the silence by quieting down. The second step is to be aware of silence in everything. It is really our awareness that listens to silence. Being aware of silence and seeing silence is the same thing. Who is aware of silence? Who sees silence? It is our enlightened nature that is aware and sees. The third step is to dwell in the clarity of silence, and once you know how to do this, the last step will be enlightening your mind and seeing your true nature. It might take quite some time to reach the third step of dwelling in the clarity of silence, but if you keep the awareness of silence, you will eventually reach it. The important thing is to keep practicing slowly and steadily. When you feel that your mind starts wandering again while listening to silence, return to step two and focus on the movement from eyes to nose to mouth to heart, with no thoughts or images in your heart.

What is our true nature? Our true nature is the emptiness of all things, the "true formless form." And Chan practice is about seeing, hearing, being aware of and clearly knowing this. That what we habitually see, hear, are aware of and know is an illusion. And so we use listening to become aware, and use awareness to realize emptiness, and then use emptiness to leave behind our mistaken views and notions. The most important point about this Chan practice of listening to silence is that it lets us enter into the true form.

The true form means the eternal—that which is unborn and never dies, which is neither stained nor pure, and neither increases nor diminishes. It is our spiritual nature, our true face before our parents were born. There is absolutely nothing here to hold on to: no rebirth in samsāra; no world of bodily form, sensation, thought, impulse or consciousness; no pain and no happiness; no gain and no loss. This is what Bodhisattva Guanyin realized through listening to the silence in the sounds of the waves. Our own practice of listening to silence is entering into the stream of our true nature and seeing our original face.

V. Listening to the Sound of an Egg

A gongan is a teaching device that helps us to break through the fetters of our conceptual and dualistic mind by raising a question that cannot be solved in a logical way. Using such a question is a practice commonly used in the Linji (Rinzai) tradition of Chan. This practice goes back all the way to the beginning when Buddha Śākyamuni lifted a flower and transmitted his teaching to Mahakāśyapā in a mind-to-mind transmission. Looking at the flower, Mahakāśyapā became enlightened. Why was the Buddha smiling? And what did Mahakāśyapā realize? If you keep contemplating these questions until you get a breakthrough, you are engaged in the work with a kōan.

Many generations after Mahakāśyapā, there was a famous and influential Chinese Chan Master by the name of Mazu Daoyi (709-788) who lived in the Tang Dynasty. Mazu loved to meditate, spending many hours sitting on a spot outside of the temple hall. One day, Master Nanjue Huairang (677-744) discovered him sitting there, fully absorbed in meditation, and thought to himself that this fellow was really serious about his meditation practice. And so Huairang picked up a tile, sat down on a rock next to Mazu and started rubbing the tile. Mazu kept meditating and Huairang kept rubbing his tile, day after day, until Mazu sighed. "This strange fellow must really have some kind of problem," he thought. "Otherwise why would he sit there rubbing a tile all the time?" And so Mazu got up from his meditation spot, walked over to Huairang and asked him, "Why in the world do you rub this tile every single day? What do you want to accomplish by this?" Huairang answered, "I am rubbing this tile to make it into a mirror." "How could you make a mirror by rubbing a tile?" Mazu asked. Huairang answered, saying, "If I cannot make a mirror by rubbing a tile, how can you achieve Buddhahood by sitting in meditation?"

Mazu was very challenged by this question and took Huairang as his teacher. After six years of study, Huairang appointed Mazu as his dharma heir , which means that he passed the mind-to-mind transmission, which goes all the way back to the Buddha and which he had received from his own teacher, the 6th Patriarch Huineng, on to his disciple Mazu.

Now let us not misunderstand this story and decide that the practice of meditation is not important. Rather, consider the fact that Mahakāśyapā had been a very serious meditator who had practiced austerities in a graveyard for many years. By devoting all of his efforts to meditation he had built up a very solid foundation for his practice. Without such a foundation, would he have become enlightened with the Buddha's lifting up of a flower? What would have happened? Nobody among the great disciples of the Buddha had any clue as to what was going on. Only Mahakāśyapā smiled. This reminds us of how important it is to build up a solid foundation for our practice.

What Huairang wanted to make clear to Mazu is that it is a misunderstanding to think that sitting all day long will result in Buddhahood. The heart and mind achieve Buddhahood in awakening, just as Mahakāśyapā did when the Buddha lifted up the flower. It's not a matter of just sitting there for many hours every day. When Huairang first saw Mazu, he must have remembered a prediction that he had received from his own Master, the 6th Patriarch, who told him that one day there would be a fine horse coming out of his stable, one that was unmatched in the whole of China. This fine horse was Mazu. When Mazu finally achieved enlightenment, he was so moved and happy that he returned back home to his village in the Southern province of Hunan to see all of his family and neighbors, intending to help them become enlightened too.

As soon as he entered his native village, all people near and far came together, since they had heard that someone who had achieved the way had entered their village. Who was the one? Big and small, they came out of their houses and stretched their necks to see him. Imagine their great surprise when they recognized Mazu—wasn't this the son of Ma Pengsuan, the young naughty boy they had all known, the one who ran all over the place without even wearing pants? Surely, he could not have the heart of a way-seeker. And so they all disbanded again. Nobody was interested in learning from Mazu, who had been so eager to share his experiences. Proclaiming that "the dharma is not fragrant at home" (in other words, "no one is a prophet in his own town") Mazu wanted to take his leave again, but his aunt held him back. "I believe in you," she said, "and I want to learn from you. Please teach me a method of meditation."

Mazu's aunt was a very busy housewife who spent the whole day in the kitchen, moving around cutting vegetables and cooking for a big family—how could she possibly engage in meditation practice in the kitchen? Mazu instructed her as follows: "Take an egg, and hang it over the stove with some string made of hemp. Listen to this egg every day, and on the day that the egg will speak to you, you will become enlightened." Mazu's aunt did exactly as he had instructed her to do and listened mindfully to the egg every single day, very careful not to miss the occasion on which the egg would speak to her and she would become enlightened. The aunt concentrated her whole being on the egg and on the moment that it would speak to her. But does an egg say anything?

An egg does not make any sound whatsoever, and as the aunt was listening, she listened to the sound of no sound—which is what we do during the Listening to Silence practice. Do you know how long the aunt listened like this moving to and fro in the kitchen every day? She listened to the egg for ten whole years, without ever forgetting that one day the egg would speak to her. Then, after ten years, the string on which the egg had been hanging broke, and the egg fell to the ground and burst with a big plop. Hearing the big plop—the sound of complete emptiness and silence—the aunt became instantly enlightened.

So if we practice the listening to silence meditation, we practice listening to the sound of the egg. Can you hear it? Listening to the sound of no sound helps us to return to our original self. This is the main point of Chan practice—the return to our original self. It is not about developing some supernatural powers, but simply this: returning home. Listening to silence is a practice that we can keep up in our busy daily lives—it is not something we only do while we are sitting on a cushion.

Our sense of hearing is active all the time, but since it is active, it is bound up with our discriminating consciousness. Contemplating a question such as "What is the sound of no sound?" or "What is the sound of one hand?" and deeply listening to the sound of silence helps us to return to that most original self that is prior to and free of all the mental distinctions that entangle us with the fleeting things of the phenomenal world.

Right now however we are not yet able to return to our original self. We are still like the spider that buries herself under so many layers of webbing that she no longer looks like a spider at all. We ourselves are wrapped up in too many activities of our consciousness, and what we need to do is to take off one layer after another to recover our original self. Listening to silence is doing that kind of job—it helps us to slowly and steadily take off the distinctions of our discriminating consciousness, removing layer upon layer of thoughts until we finally arrive home. If we carry too many things with us, our consciousness remains so layered with things that it becomes the very things it is wrapped up with.

When we listen to silence, we eliminate the connection to everything that is not quiet. Listening to silence is like cutting the electricity so that the light of our discriminating consciousness is no longer a distraction. What remains in the end is the listening heart. The most important thing in our practice is to recover that very heart.

SUMMARY AND CONCLUSION TRANSFORMING YOURSELF AND THE WORLD: CHAN MEDITATION IN DAILY PRACTICE

In taking the path of Chan, we usually speak about four basic steps, which are: trust, understanding, practice and realization. First, we have to trust that the practice of Chan is good and helpful for us. This trust makes us interested in studying Buddhism and learning everything about Chan. The benefits of meditation are well-known. It improves our health by regulating our breathing and energizing our blood circulation. People who meditate on a regular basis can live longer, just like the famous Master Zhaozhou (778-897) who reached the ripe age of 120 years old. Meditation helps us to deepen our mental concentration and stabilize our bodies and minds. It lets us return to our true self and find inner peace.

But in order to practice meditation, we need to understand the method of Chan practice and see it in the context of the teaching of the Buddha. Does the teaching make sense to us, or are there still some areas that we need to study more systematically in order to get a more complete understanding? After we have finished our initial study and arrived at some understanding of what Buddhism and Chan are all about, we need to start putting it into practice in our daily lives. This is the only way for us to understand and experience how Chan helps and benefits us in our daily life. It is the only way to reach realization.

In our practice we have to proceed like an explorer who enters more and more deeply into new territory. Our exploration leads us to a very refined understanding of the relationship between the mind and the material world. When we observe the many constant changes of our body, feelings and thoughts, when we realize the impermanence of the things of the material world that entrap us, then we are able to let go and enter more deeply into inner exploration until our mind becomes as clear as a mirror that reflects everything equally and impartially. When we continue further in our exploration we will discover that which has been there from the beginning, that eternal spiritual existence which transcends the round of birth and death—our original face.

However, usually the time that we can set apart for practice is very limited, while the time that we spend on our daily activities is plentiful. That is the reason why we have to learn how to bring our practice into our daily lives. Otherwise we would be wasting a lot of precious time for our exploration. Let us bring our practice into the reality of our ordinary lives, and let us bring our ordinary lives into the reality of our practice. If we can do this, there will no longer be a contradiction between life and practice. For many people, even for our nuns and monks in the monastery, there often remains a gap between daily life and practice that they find difficult to overcome. But there is no such gap in my teaching, in which I always emphasize that Chan is life and that life is Chan. It is in our daily lives that we search for truth and understanding; it is here that we strive to enlighten our heart and mind and see our true nature. When we bring Chan into every activity of our daily lives, our space that felt so narrow and constricted before becomes more and more expansive.

Chan is not just what we just do on our cushions. In Chan we speak about the four bodily postures: walking, standing, sitting and lying down. While it is important to keep a daily practice of seated meditation, the practice continues in all other bodily positions that we take during the course of a day, not just during sitting. The most important thing is to always come back to the here and now and not get lost in our memories of the past or our anxieties about the future. Our life is always happening in the here and now, and this is where our practice happens as well, from moment to moment.

As you know by now, when I first took the path of Chan I secluded myself from the busy world outside to devote myself entirely to my exploration. It was eerily quiet in the old, dilapidated pagoda where I first started my practice after becoming a monk. I could not hear any other person's voice there the whole day long, and after a few days this overwhelming quietness made me feel incredibly uneasy and restless. Especially at night, the whole world seemed so desolate and deserted that it was frightening. At that time, I only had one thought left in my mind: I want to be together with other people; I want to talk to them! I did not know how to cope with this loneliness that enveloped me like never before.

In this situation, my mind was constantly troubled by contradictory and conflicting thoughts, but I knew that I had to face my loneliness if I wanted to overcome my troubles and fears. The only way to make some progress in my practice was to go on and not give up. And so I continued the battle with my self-centered thoughts, my longings, my likes and dislikes and my wrong ideas. Finally one evening, after finishing one round of sitting, I came to feel a deep and calm inner peace, in which all those feelings of fear and even terror of the night had completely vanished. I realized with overwhelming clarity that if my mind and heart are completely free from attachment, then there is absolutely nothing left that can produce any fear or terror! When my heart is as clear and bright as a mirror, it freely reflects everything without anyone remaining there to be affected by the reflections. This state is the unconditional and unlimited freedom of the spirit, the true nature of our heart and mind.

This true nature is eternal and luminous. It is unchanging, all-pervasive and all-present. When we awaken to it we experience true peace for the very first time. And with that, we come to feel unlimited love and compassion for all beings. This is my personal experience of Chan.

As my practice continued in the graveyard and still later in the cave, I gained more and more insight into the problem of life and death and suffering. As my insight deepened, I could hear a voice within me which kept saying, "You have to help others through the teaching of Buddhism. Share everything that you have experienced and realized through your Chan practice with them." And so I decided to return to the world and to make daily life among others my place for continued practice.

And even though I changed my way of life—from practice in total seclusion to practice in the midst of the world, that which has not changed at all is the importance that daily Chan practice has for me. For example, in the ten-year period when we built the Museum of World Religions, I never forgot my daily practice of seated meditation, even though our work for the museum was challenging and seemed never-ending. Even if I only had a short amount of time in which to do it, I sat at least once every day to let my thoughts come to rest and clarity and to be able to face the new challenges.

The practice of Chan gives us energy, and this has to do with the power of enlightenment. In meditation, we are constantly attentive to what is happening inside us. Our meditation is based on the trust that we can touch and unleash the power of enlightenment, and that this power will help us to constantly transcend our self-centered lives. The practice of Chan gives us deep insight into our heart and mind. The true nature of the mind is the nature of the universe, the dharma-nature. If we understand this true nature, we understand everything in the universe. If we are not able to understand the true nature of our heart and minds we are not able to understand everything in the universe. And even though the practice of Chan focuses on that which is inside us, in the very end, there is no difference whatsoever between what is inside and outside us. Meditation means opening up to the life of the universe and becoming one with it. It means leading an authentic life. If we can constantly deepen and transform our awareness in daily life, then every single day of our life is a new life and a new beginning, full of unspent energy.

The greatest difference between the awareness that is created through Chan meditation and the rational, discursive approach has to do with how we see external things or phenomena. In the rational, discursive approach we are often influenced by the things that we analyze. Thus, we are in no position to find out the meaning behind it all. Chan is different. It lets us illuminate our mind and see our true nature, which means that we can understand the meaning behind things. Chan also teaches us how we should deal with external things. This does not mean that the discursive, rational approach is not necessary or important. On the contrary, both complement each other. Or to express it in the language of Buddhism, they are related like the inner principle (ti) and the outer application (yung) or like transcendence and immanence. We need both to be complete.

It is similar with the relationship between meditation and emotions, which is also a relationship between inner principle and outer application. Chan meditation teaches us not to be overwhelmed by our feelings. Buddhism teaches us that all sentient beings experience suffering. Chan meditation helps us to transcend the suffering that is tied to our emotions. We all live in this world together. If we are not able to constantly purify our self-centered feelings, then it becomes be very difficult for us to live or work together with others. The practice of Chan helps us to purify our emotions. It helps us to "refrain from doing what is unwholesome and to do what is wholesome." Purified emotions are the best basis from which to cope with daily life in this world. In Buddhism, this basis is called "unconditional love" or "great compassion."

The practice of Chan helps us to open up the treasure house of unused potentials within us. As you know clearly by now, the main goal of this practice is to develop the power of enlightenment and return home to our true self. If we are able to develop this power and return home, the treasure house will completely open up by itself. Again, the way to accomplish this is by practicing the two principal methods that I explained earlier: stopping (shamatā) and seeing (vipassanā). Sitting in meditation settles our body and mind and stops the incessant flow of distractive thoughts. When our body and mind are settled, we engage in contemplation by practicing deep listening. In deep listening to silence we contemplate the unborn nature of our own heart. Listening to silence awakens the power of enlightenment within us and lets us see everything in the universe with new eyes, unleashing the flow of unconditional love and compassion.

But from my own experience I need to say a word of caution here. Chan meditation which is not based on the right method can go wrong. We can liken the practice of Chan to a battle. If we are not careful along the way, especially when we have not yet reached the true liberation which is the goal of this battle, our carelessness might do damage to our practice. Therefore please be careful to practice under the guidance of an experienced teacher and in accordance with the prescribed method.

Through meditation we come to clearly know that we and all living beings form one living body—that they are not different from me and I am not different from them. There is no way for us to separate ourselves from this shared living body, or to split it up into disconnected parts. And since this is so, we will very naturally respond to everyone we meet and everything that happens with a compassionate and loving heart. This is an experience that grows very naturally out of Chan practice. We can of course use many words to describe this, but if we want to really know and experience it, we have to do the practice.

We all live in this deeply interconnected world together. If we have not learned to constantly purify our own selfish feelings, then we will not succeed in living or working together in peace and harmony. The practice of Chan helps us to clarify and purify our feelings until we are really able to embody Bodhisattva Guanyin's unconditional love and great compassion ourselves.

In closing, let me bring up again my experience from the time when I was practicing meditation in the graveyard. In Asia, and in many other places, everybody fears and abhors roaming spirits and ghosts. In the course of my own practice, I developed a deeper sense of compassion, and with that I understood that these spirits are suffering beings in the circle of life, death and rebirth. And so a thought took hold of me — I wanted to help them. This so completely transformed my originally hostile attitude, that we became friends and got along peacefully. If this is possible with spirits, then how much more so is it possible with living human beings.

If we can practice Chan and manage to completely dissolve all blockages and hindrances of our heart and mind, if we can find inner peace, if we can see through all forms of life in this universe and realize that we all together form one single body, then we can let go of our hang-ups and live together in peace and love. In my case, the teaching of Buddhism and the experience of Chan led me to found a monastery and build the Museum of World Religions. The museum is my contribution to a loving and peaceful global family which comes straight from the heart. My wish and prayer is that this little book will be of help in guiding you to return home to your heart and open wide the treasures that are hidden there. When your heart is at peace, the world will be at peace.

Ven. Dharma Master Hsin Tao,

Abbot and Founder of the Wu Sheng Monastery in Ling Jiou Mountain, is internationally renowned for having established the Museum of World Religions in Taipei, Taiwan, and for his unceasing efforts to bring about world peace through mutual understanding and dialogue among religions. His continuing promotion of world peace after the tragedy of the Twin Towers disaster in New York City through multifaceted initiatives including a series of Buddhist-Muslim and interfaith dialogues held in many countries around the world between 2002 and 2015 has earned him global recognition as a world religious leader. Master Hsin Tao received Dharma Transmission from Master Ben-huan of the Hongfa Temple in China, becoming the 5th successor in the Linji Chan Tradition. He has more than thirty volumes of published works in Chinese, and some works in German and English.

Maria Reis Habito,

International Program Director of the Museum of World Religions based in Taipei, Taiwan, and also Director of the Elijah Interfaith Institute USA, completed her Ph.D. in East Asian Studies and Philosophy at the University of Munich in 1990. She practiced Zen under Yamada Koun Roshi of the Sanbo Zen Tradition and was appointed a Zen teacher in 2008, leading practice groups in Dallas, Texas and South Bend, Indiana. A longtime disciple of Master Hsin Tao, Maria also works as his translator, and accompanies him on his teachings tours around the world. Her publications include 2 books in German, 2 books in English, and numerous scholarly articles on Buddhist and Interfaith themes. She lives in Dallas, and is married with two young adult sons.

CPSIA information can be obtained
at www.ICGtesting.com
Printed in the USA
BVHW041222181218
535877BV00020B/3692/P

9 781530 660131